Children of the Street

Teaching in the Inner-City

DOROTHY J. SKEEL
Indiana University

LIBRARY
University of Texas
At San Antonio

WITHDRAWN
UTSA Libraries

Goodyear Publishing Company, Inc.
Pacific Palisades, California

© 1971 by Goodyear Publishing Company, Inc.
Pacific Palisades, California

Y-180X-0

Current printing (last number):
10 9 8 7 6 5 4 3 2 1

ISBN: 0-87620-180-X

Library of Congress Catalog Card No.:   76-144842

Printed in the United States of America

To those children whose lives have been blighted by their environment—hopefully the environment can be improved, but certainly their education should help them overcome the obstacles.

Contents

Preface

Anyone who has experienced the honest, sincere trust of a child—any child—should squirm when confronted with the tragic statistics of the achievement levels of inner-city children. Children depend upon adults to provide them with an adequate education that will prepare them to live useful and purposeful lives. Where have we failed inner-city children? The massive school systems required by our bulging cities are faced with the tremendous problem of impersonalization—administrative policies that affect thousands of children are made in the central office without adequate knowledge of these children. But the most crucial problem facing these schools is the lack of teachers adequately prepared to teach in inner-city schools. This book is an attempt to give pre-service and in-service elementary teachers some practical suggestions to improve instruction in their inner-city classrooms.

Terms such as "disadvantaged," "culturally-deprived," and "lower socio-economic" are applied to inner-city populations. These terms may be found in the text when quotes are taken from other sources. The author applies the term "inner-city" to the thousands of children who are affected educationally by the crowded and sub-standard living conditions of many of our inner-city cores. These children may be black, white, yellow, red, or brown, and may belong to any number of ethnic groups.

The first section of the book discusses the tremendous problems of environment and an inadequate educational system facing inner-city children. It then goes on to the portrait of a good teacher, how he should be trained, and the instructional and organizational considerations that should be made in the classroom. The next section describes teaching techniques for reading and language art, social studies, math and science, and the arts and physical education. The author believes that many inner-city teachers could provide a better educational environment for children if they had sufficient knowledge of instructional practices that produce the desired results. Hopefully this book will contribute to that end.

This book is based on an earlier chapter, "Teaching the Disadvantaged," that appears in *The Challenge of Teaching Social Studies in the Elementary School*, published by Goodyear Publishing Company, Inc.

Many people assist an author in the preparation of a book, but I specifically wish to acknowledge James P. Levy and Karen Christenson for their advice and consultation; Cynthia Jemsek for her support; and Marsha Magnuson for her expert assistance in the preparation of the manuscript.

Children of the Street

A child hides behind a car in the tenement street of a large city. He watches the gang of boys approaching and shakes with fright. If they catch him, he knows what will happen since he has ratted on the gang. Where can he turn for help? His parents are both away working, there's a wino sprawled in the doorway of the house next door, but otherwise the street is deserted. Would anyone heed his call for help, but more important to him, would he be labeled a weakling-coward if he asked for help? As the gang comes closer, he knows they have spotted him. . . .

Tim appears in school the next morning with the physical scars of the fight quite visible, but even more apparent are the scars on the inside as revealed in his eyes. What happens to a child such as this when he sits in a strict and disciplined atmosphere all day with no release for his hurt feelings and the hatred building up inside? How can he concentrate on his reading? Who cares where sweet, clean, little Jane is going? No one seems to care that he has been hurt—even his mother yelled at him for getting into a fight, and the teacher just looked at him. Unfortunately the circumstances of Tim's life are not alike those of many children living in urban environments.

Let's look at the environmental backgrounds of a group of children

1

found in a typical *third*-grade urban classroom. There's Bobby, who
is Tim's good friend. Bobby is one of the class troublemakers—anyway,
that's what the teacher says. Bobby isn't interested in much that's going
on in the classroom. He's busy poking Sam, who's sitting next to him,
and crawling along the floor to take away Kip's book. Bobby never
seems to sit still, but then why should he, he never gets the chance
to have a chair at home, there're too many children. Bobby refers to
his mother as Miss Lilly, a woman who has never legally married any
of the fathers of her seven children. Bobby has no idea who his father
is and the only emotional security he receives is from his grandmother,
who lives with them. Bobby tries to be a big shot and get as much
attention from his classmates as possible. His daily trips to the principal's
office give him some security and a male relationship.

Barbara is a thin, quiet girl who never disturbs anyone; nor does
she participate in class activities. Her parents have recently moved
from the Southern mountains and have not adjusted to the ways of
urban life. Barbara doesn't read very well and therefore has to use
one of those baby books. Her father is always teasing her about it,
but he only went through the sixth grade and can't read much better.
There are six docile children in the family and the father dominates
the home life completely. Barbara's mother is fearful of her husband
and has very little to say.

Sheila is a bright-eyed, gregarious girl who must know about everything that is going on. She is the class busybody—watching and tattling.
There's a large family at home: her mother, father, four children, and
an aunt and uncle with their three children. Sheila has an older sister
who is going to have a baby, even though she is only fourteen. Sheila
knows all about how it happened because she was watching her sister
and one of the neighborhood boys in bed. Sheila was going to tell
her mother about it, but her sister, who takes care of the younger
kids, promised Sheila she could watch the late movie on TV every
night. Sheila liked this idea because there were too many kids in bed
anyway. Sheila tries to take a nap in school, but the teacher is always
hollering at her.

Lacey is a self-conscious boy, big for his age, who stands well
above the other children. His size has forced him into trouble many
times. Lacey's mother and father are quiet, hard-working people, wh
take good care of their only child. Unfortunately, Lacey's size and h
neighborhood environment have forced him into joining a gang of ol

boys for protection—the gang that beat up Tim. Lacey's gang had gone over into the next neighborhood and robbed a grocery store. Tim had seen them do it and told Lacey's parents, who couldn't believe their boy would do such a thing. And of course Lacey denied it when his parents confronted him. The storekeeper was badly hurt, but would live.

That's just a sampling of the children found in almost any urban classroom. How does a teacher handle such problems? There's little she can do about her students' environmental backgrounds.

Numerous educators have advocated that urban children who come from such chaotic home environments need structure, orderliness and discipline in their educational environments. What does a structured, orderly, disciplined classroom accomplish for the Bobbys, Barbaras, Tims, Sheilas, and Laceys? How do they survive? To use an old cliche, "It's like trying to force a round peg in a square hole." Let's follow Bobby through a typical day in this type of educational environment.

Bobby starts off the day in the slow-reading group (he can't read) and before anything is accomplished, he is sent back to his seat for misbehaving. He quickly begins to bother Tim, who is in the next reading group and is trying to finish his workbook. Before too long Bobby is sent out in the hall, where he pesters everyone who walks by. He stays there until recess time, when he successfully causes enough trouble on the playground to be sent to the principal's office. He waits there because the principal has many children to discipline. After the principal's usual chat about not pushing the little kids and his spanking (the principal believes you have to hit them to make them understand), Bobby goes back to the classroom in time for a spelling test. But Bobby was in the principal's office yesterday at spelling time and doesn't know the words. His teacher hollers at him constantly during the test and breathes a sigh of relief when his reading tutor appears at the door for him.

Bobby spends the fifteen-minute tutoring time conning the tutor (a young college student who has had no training) into believing that his eyes bother him and he can't possibly read—yesterday he had a headache. By the time he has finished the discussion with his tutor, it's time for lunch. After lunch it's social studies time and the class is assigned to read a chapter in the book. Of course, Bobby can't read, and the teacher provides nothing else for the nonreaders. Bobby spends the time drawing on the pictures in the book and promptly receives a reprimand from the teacher. He is required to take a large eraser and go to the back of the room so he won't disturb the social studies discussion (the one time he might understand something). As he tears the book in the erasing process, the teacher calls everyone's attention to his clumsiness.

The school day is finished off with some language-study exercises which sound pretty dumb to Bobby. What has he accomplished in school today? Nothing, and the teacher is totally frustrated by her attempts to make Bobby fit the pattern of what she thinks are well-structured instructional experiences. But let's face it, Bobby doesn't fit the pattern. Unfortunately too many Bobbys spend their schoolday this way.

One young teacher in an urban school remarked during her second year of teaching, "I don't know what educational activities you'll see going on in my room, but those children are well disciplined [first-graders]."

As one visits an inner-city school operating on this philosophical basis, one feels an air of tension. It's like trying to keep the lid on a can of dynamite. The older the children become, the more one is aware of the tension within them. Obviously it must be released sometime, either in the street, or, as often happens, in school at the junior- and senior-high levels. Why can't the energy be channeled into worthwhile and productive activities?

Another serious problem that encumbers the urban child is his negative self-concept. In the description of the home environments, it is obvious why such feelings would develop. Parents have too many children, are working hard to support them and therefore have little time to spend with the children. The discipline is immediate and physical in order to solve the problem as soon as possible. In the impersonal world of the city, the child is overwhelmed and does not develop the feeling that he is important or worthwhile to anyone.

Frequently the gang on the street replaces the family group and the value system of the gang is adopted.[1] This means that the group (or gang) is more vital than the individual. When the child reaches school, once again what is imposed upon him is done for the welfare of the group and not the individual. Also many of these children are members of minority groups who may not be accepted outside their immediate community. Frequently they encounter teachers in the

[1] A. Harry Passow, ed., *Education in Depressed Areas* (New York: Teachers College Publications, 1963), p. 113.

schools who are prejudiced toward them. However, this does not mean that these aren't children with intense feelings and desires. They do not arrive at school expecting to fail. Most of these children are curious, outgoing youngsters who want somebody and something to believe in. Adults in their world have in many cases failed them miserably. Unless the teacher is an understanding and reliable individual who believes in these children and their ability to learn, once again the adult world has failed them.

When inner-city children were asked what they liked about teachers, responses such as these were made: "She's our friend." "She's nice to us." "She doesn't give as much homework." "She doesn't hit us." "He lets us go out to recess even when we are bad." "We have science with him." "She plays games with us." "She's softer." In asking these same children what they disliked about teachers, they replied: "She hollers too much." "She fusses at us." "She picks on Webster and makes him sit up front." "She makes us pay attention." "She makes us sit too quiet."

The picture of likes and dislikes is quite revealing. Do the teachers' characteristics sound different from what *any* child would want to find in a teacher? Why do teachers have so much difficulty with inner-city children? Teachers find three basic problems in their adjustment to teaching these children: (1) presenting learning experiences (2) discipline (3) moral acceptability.[2] Teachers who are forced into inner-city situations react negatively toward these children and responses frequently heard are: "I just don't understand them." "They simply won't sit still." "They're fine individually, but as a group!" "If you're nice to these children, they take advantage of you, or they take it as a sign of weakness." What effect do teachers with attitudes such as these have on the development of a positive self-concept?

The environmental experiences of inner-city children prior to the time they enter school do not prepare them for the typical Dick, Jane, Mac and Muff type of instructional experience. Much of the vocabulary used by the teacher and found in the instructional materials is not understandable to them. This does not mean they can't learn. It's very much like the visitor from a foreign country who speaks limited English and doesn't know the jargon. He appears less intelligent and doesn't catch on as quickly. Thus the inner-city child faces the same problem.

---

[2]Howard S. Becker, "Social Class Variations in the Teacher-Pupil Relationship," *Journal of Educational Sociology* XXV (April, 1952), 452–54.

However there is a conflict—do you continue to reinforce his present language or do you present instructional experiences that help him to understand new language? Educators cannot agree about using dialect and the language of the street to teach these children to read. It is quite obvious, though, that the teacher must understand the child's language to communicate with him.

So often a bleak picture of the inner-city child is presented without the positive factors of the environment recognized. These positive factors include: an interest in vocational education; parents' and children's respect for education in spite of their dislike for school, where they sense a resentment of them; the children's slow cognitive style of learning, hidden verbal talent, freedom from self-blame and parental over-protection, lack of sibling rivalry, informality, humor and enjoyment of music, games and sports.[3] These positives may provide a basis on which teachers can build a more adequate educational program.

Knowing the needs of the inner-city child, his experiences and the positive factors from his environment will lay the framework within which the teachers should operate. Now it is time to look at the portrait of a good teacher, classroom conditions and organizations and the role of the child to provide the best education for the inner-city child.

---

[3]Frank Riessman, "The Culturally Deprived Child: A New View," *School Life* XLV (April, 1963), 57.

Portrait of a Teacher

Miss Sims is a sensitive and responsive young woman, who teaches a first grade in an inner-city school. The school is dull grey stone and quite unattractive, with a high cyclone fence around it. The rooms are large, with high ceilings, plenty of blackboards, but little storage space. The desks are old and scarred from previous occupants. But these drab surroundings are not noticed by the children as they enter the school and their classroom. Why? For many reasons, but most importantly because Miss Sims is greeting each child with a smile and a question or comment for each individual. The smile isn't forced and as each child looks into her face, he sees the interest and sometimes the concern in her eyes.

Let's listen to her for a minute as she greets the children.

"Sarah, what a pretty dress, you must be proud of it." The child beams and nods her head even though it's apparent the dress is too large for her and probably was handed down from her older sister. That really doesn't matter; the important fact is her teacher noticed she had a new dress and is interested enough in her to tell her so.

The next child who entered was a frail little boy clutching a brown paper bag.

"Juan, do you have a surprise for us?" queried the teacher.

"Yes," and he promptly dumped an array of stones collected from the beach.

"Well, you're going to have some interesting experiences to tell us this morning. Do you want to tell me now or should I wait until the other children hear it?"

Juan said, "Oh, no! I'll tell you now. See these stones?"

"Did you get them at the beach?" asked the teacher.

"No, why? I traded with Steve next door. He got a couple of my marbles. Aren't these pretty?"

"Yes, they are pretty. Someone collected them at the beach. Do you know why I know that?"

"No, how can you tell?"

"See how round and smooth they are? They've been washed over by the water and rolled and rolled. Do you want to look in the book, and we'll find the names to call them?"

"Now I can tell the kids all about them!"

At that moment Charles dashed into the room with Sylvia close at his heels. Charles raced for the security and protection of the teacher, announcing loudly, "Sylvia has bugs, Sylvia has bugs." The teacher knew in truth Sylvia did have lice, but she also knew that the little girl could not help it and needed her support. Sylvia had a bath several times a month at school, but continued to be reinfected at home. Miss Sims put her arms around the crying Sylvia and gave a quiet reprimand to Charles for his rudeness. "Charles, why do you pick on other people? Would you want people to call you names or say things about you?"

"But Sylvia does have bugs."

"That doesn't make any difference, you don't have any right to tell everyone about it." The teacher didn't try to deny the fact that Sylvia had lice, but rather how wrong Charles was to tease her about it.

In these few examples has Miss Sims done anything different from what most good teachers would do when greeting a group of first-graders in the morning? Not really. The difference is that Miss Sims accepted these children as they were—she knew Sarah's dress wasn't new, but it was important to Sarah; she knew Juan had never been farther away from his home than school; she knew Sylvia had lice and that Charles knew it, but didn't give him the right to tease her about it. The children knew Miss Sims liked, respected and was interested in them. They in turn felt the same way about her.

What type of classroom procedures does Miss Sims use with these children? In the morning when the children arrived, they were excited and wanted to share discussion with her and the other children, so there was time set aside for this. Juan discussed his rock collection adding more information as a result of his talk with Miss Sims. Billy described a bad fight on his block that had upset him. Miss Sims didn't try to stop him; rather, she used the opportunity to talk about why people fight, if the children engaged in fighting, and how they feel when they fight. The teacher didn't moralize about fighting, telling the children never to do it, but they discussed when a fight might be necessary, and when it wasn't.

After the children were talked out (which often takes a longer time), Miss Sims used the topics from the discussion for a language experience chart. The chart provided the basis for their morning reading instruction and their writing. The children read the chart and added pictures for the words that were difficult for them. Each child copied the chart and chose some part of it (his favorite) to illustrate. While the entire group was completing this task, Miss Sims took each child individually for reading instruction. Matthew was constructing a story of his own that the teacher was typing for him. When it was finished, he would illustrate it and place it on the library table for others to read. Not every child was ready to do this; some were unable to reconstruct the sequence of a story. These children as a group were looking at a series of pictures and describing and sequencing the events. These are typical readiness activities, but the difference was that Miss Sims was using actual photographs of people and happenings in their community—these pictures were within the experiences of the children.

When the children came back from recess Miss Sims read a story to quiet them after their boisterous activities on the playground. She knew they needed the experience of someone reading to them since many did not receive it within their homes due to the lack of books and limited spare time of their working parents. She was pleased to see Craig listening for a change; he was a hyperactive child and frequently wandered around the room investigating the interest centers while she was reading. She had never reprimanded Craig for doing this since she knew he couldn't sit still for very long.

The remainder of the morning was spent in active participation with math materials. The children had wooden blocks and puzzles that could be handled to complete their addition facts and recognize geometric shapes. Miss Sims worked with a small group of children at a time, but gave individual encouragement when needed.

After lunch the children assembled in their chairs close around Miss Sims. She had some social studies discussion pictures to share with them. This series depicted children (much like them in ages and races) with different emotions expressed after typical childlike problems. Miss Sims had the children tell her about the pictures, how the children felt, if they had ever felt the same way, what could be done to solve the problems. Miss Sims was very careful to permit the children to express descriptions of their own experiences. She listened carefully and answered questions when necessary. This activity increased the children's oral language facility as well as serving as an outlet for their emotions. When this activity was completed, the children played a short game which permitted freedom of movement and expression.

The last activity of the day was science; the children were excited because today was the day they were to weigh their gerbils to see if the proper food had helped them gain weight. They told Miss Sims what to write on the experience chart about the animals, what they had fed them and how much weight the animals had gained.

Before each child left for the day, he had a brief conference with Miss Sims about what had been done today and what he had learned. While these conferences were going on, the other children chose something to do from the interest centers or completed any activities they had not completed during the day.

And of course Miss Sims was there to say good-bye to each child as he left. What a satisfying day for the children and the teacher. There had been minor discipline problems during the day, but these had been handled calmly and quietly. There had been plenty of activities for the children to express themselves orally and also experiences that permitted them to move about the room. School was a stimulating experience for these inner-city children.

What was different about the teacher? The teacher understood and was sincerely interested in the children's problems. She was a person who could be trusted. She was cognizant of the most effective teaching techniques for these children. Research indicates that the following factors[4] should be considered in planning educational programs for them:

(1) Children's interest and concern for the here and now;

(2) Extensive concrete examples are necessary for their cognitive style of perception and learning;

(3) The children experience difficulty in classifying, relating and integrating knowledge;

(4) Learning is most successful when the process is self-involving and of an active nature;

(5) The teacher should show an expectation of success;

(6) Repetition of information is necessary through a variety of approaches;

(7) There should be continuous feedback to the student on his progress.

Also, she was willing to accept the children as they were and help them learn as much as possible. The teacher never discredited the values, beliefs and customs of the children's culture, but did make them aware that other people behaved differently. She was an important link between home and school and related the learning experiences to the children's environments. As their teacher she provided the important motivation for learning that is often lacking in their home environment.

HOW SHOULD TEACHERS BE PREPARED TO TEACH IN THE INNER-CITY?

Earlier in this text a young (second year) teacher was quoted as saying, "I don't know what educational activities you'll see going on, but it is a well-disciplined room." How had this young teacher arrived at the conclusion that good teaching was synonymous with a well-disciplined classroom? In her teacher-education preparation? In the sub-social system of the school? In her own schooling background?

---

[4]Staten W. Webster, ed., *The Disadvantaged Learner: Knowing, Understanding, Educating* (San Francisco, Calif.: Chandler Publishing Co., 1966), p. 477. An INTEXT Publisher.

Probably all three areas provided some reinforcement for the idea. Her teacher preparation may have espoused a different approach, but since it was not provided in a realistic setting, there was little opportunity for practical application (methods courses, practical experiences, and student teaching in suburbia). Then, armed with this preparation, she entered a school system filled with administrators and experienced teachers who believed and supported the theory: "A good classroom is a quiet classroom. Inner-city children need quiet, structured classrooms to overcome their chaotic environments."

How long can an inexperienced teacher (no matter how idealistic) withstand the pressures of the status quo? Teachers who do withstand these pressures (the percentage is small) and conduct their classes with freedom of thought and movement are frequently ostracized by their administrators and fellow teachers. After observing one young man who had obviously reached his children, and they were enjoying the experience, the principal remarked how unorthodox his teaching procedures were. One is tempted to throw up one's hands until it is realized that thousands—no, possibly millions—of children are exposed to this type of classroom atmosphere daily. Certainly such teacher behavior is not confined to inner-city schools. All one need do is read John Holt's *Why Children Fail*, Herbert Kohl's *36 Children*, Jonathan Kozol's *Death at an Early Age*. But why have these books had so little impact in changing the status quo? Much of the blame can be placed at the doorstep of the university. Such meager attempts have been made to improve the training of teachers for inner-city schools. What should be done? Three areas of concern identified are: (1) selection of teachers; (2) change in training practices; (3) more adequate in-service education.

Selection of Teachers

Instruments need to be designed to assist in the selection of teachers who would be trained for inner-city schools. A recent study found that a "Cultural Attitude Inventory" was significant. To select student teachers who were successful with inner-city children, the inventory required reactions to statements such as:

> Children from disadvantaged homes need socialization experiences, but time in school should not be wasted on these experiences.

Disadvantaged children should not be given help, but be taught as other children.

Teachers should respect disadvantaged children rather than pity or love them.[5]

Not every individual, no matter how much he may desire it, is capable of working with inner-city children. Unconscious racial prejudice (since there is a large majority of blacks in inner-city), lack of congruence with the children's cultural backgrounds and an inability to cope with the system would be the major handicaps. Teachers with years of experience repeatedly " transfer out " of the difficult schools. The reasons most often given for transfer requests have been identified as the teacher's incompatibility with the " personality peculiarities."[6] Possession of missionary zeal is not sufficient reason to teach in inner-city schools. To be effective, teachers need the crucial ingredient of a basic human respect.[7] Feeling sorry for these children isn't the way to reach them. Rather a respect for them and an enjoyment of their spirit and responsive nature would serve better. The fact that the supply and demand for teachers is now about equal may force the issue of selection processes. There is still the concern that the less effective preservice teacher will be hired for the inner-city schools.

Change in Training Practices

Typically a college professor teaching a methods course lectures on the teaching techniques and materials that should produce good results in the classroom. How unrealistic!! Frequently the student doesn't see a classroom until sometime in the future when he does his student teaching. Then whom does he ask if the particular method doesn't work? He asks his cooperating or supervising teacher, who isn't familiar with the technique and prefers to go by the book. And so the student acqui-

---

[5]Dorothy J. Skeel, "Determining the Compatibility of Student Teachers for Culturally Deprived Areas by Means of a Cultural Attitude Inventory." (Doctoral Dissertation, Pennsylvania State University, 1966).

[6]Patrick J. Groff, "Dissatisfaction in Teaching the CD Child," *Phi Delta Kappan* XLV (November, 1963), 76.

[7]Frank Riessman and A. Hannah, "Big-City School: Problems and Prospects," *Parent Teacher Magazine* LIX (November, 1964), 14.

esces and goes by the book. What remains of the impact of the methods course? Very little.

How can this practice be changed? An interesting attempt is being made by a TTT Project (government-funded Training of Teacher Trainers, Indiana University). The university professor teaches his methods courses in one of the local public schools. This also occurs in an inner-city school about fifty miles away from the campus. The student stays in the school to observe and to practice the teaching techniques immediately. Student teaching is taken concurrently with the methods. The professor is also available for feedback on the success or failure of the methods. In addition, the methods professor is in the classrooms daily to see whether the methods he espouses are realistic for the school setting. At the same time the cooperating teachers are receiving instruction in seminars on the new materials and teaching strategies so they may demonstrate these in their classrooms for the preservice teacher. Does it work? Yes, to the extent it has been attempted. Does it have problems? Yes. How many university professors want to leave or can afford (promotion-wise) to leave the campus and immerse themselves in the problems and anxieties of the public schools? On the other hand, how many public school administrators and teachers want university-oriented professors housed in their public school classrooms? Actually this may be a more workable solution than most educators would admit. Fortunately students are becoming stronger in their protest cries for a relevant education, which may force the universities, colleges and public schools into action.

There are other changes that must be made in teacher preparation in addition to the above-mentioned methods instruction. Earlier experiences in the schools, community involvement, course work in urban culture, geography, social change and value systems will provide the preservice teacher with adequate knowledge and understanding of the urban environment. Too frequently universities do not have trained faculty to provide such courses. Here the university overlooks the resources of the community. What better place to learn about the problems and culture of urban life than in the laboratory of the city? Certainly the college student needs more than the practical experiences, but there should be a balance between the practical and theoretical.

Cuban sees the teacher's role as including three facets: a decision-maker in the classroom, creating and choosing curriculum materials and being an active participant in the community. "But of the three facets of the teacher's role . . . the time spent in personal contact with parents and members of the community enriches both instruction and curriculum development. Cut off from this function, the classroom becomes pedestrian and irrelevant; the community loses the human touch that schools can ill afford to scrap."[8] Unfortunately little change will occur unless a sufficient number of people in the power positions of our universities, colleges and public schools are committed to making a change for the better in the preparation of teachers for the inner-city schools.

In-Service Education

What about the teachers already teaching in the inner-city schools? There are many fine, responsive teachers in the inner-city, but others have not moved away from the concept of the teacher as an information giver. Too many are concerned with subjects, not children. Melby believes that the traditional lesson-bound, subject-oriented teacher is most inadequate with these children. These teachers " . . . have little faith in human potential, little sympathy with those whom our vast industrial machine has spewed out as unusable and—worst of all—little love for children."[9]

But how can the behavior of these teachers be changed? Talking about changes in instructional procedures, curriculum materials and the importance of community involvement isn't sufficient. What effect will this have on a teacher who for years has been exhibiting different behavior in and out of the classroom? The in-service instruction mentioned in the TTT Project is an example of the time needed to work with teachers. A day or two-day workshop at the beginning or middle of the year doesn't accomplish much in changing behavior as do the day-to-day contacts of university–public school personnel. It takes time for trust between the two groups to be built before any real changes in behavior will occur. Not every school and university can sponsor a TTT Project, but the working relationship can be established from

[8]Larry Cuban, *To Make A Difference: Teaching in the Inner-City* (New York: The Free Press, 1970), p. 239.
[9]Ernest O. Melby, *The Teacher and Learning* (Washington: The Center for Applied Research in Education, 1963), p. 8.

funds of both groups. Dual appointments between public school and university might be more effective.

The teacher to be immersed in the community, able to communicate with parents from the inner-city, may require the development of communication workshops. These workshops would include parents, teachers and administrators. This would provide the opportunity to sit down and listen (not always talking) to parents discuss what it is they want for their children in education. Quickly, someone will point out, parents aren't interested, we only had ten out for PTA last month. As much as some PTAs have done for inner-city schools, they do not always reach the low-income parents. Many of these parents feel they are not articulate enough and adequately dressed to attend PTA meetings. In a communication workshop (not held at school, but in some community building and facilitated by a National Laboratory Trainer) parents, teachers and administrators are on a more equal footing. Definitely let's not forget administrators, since changes in teacher behavior may not receive full fruition unless principals and administrators are equally involved.

Through the evolution of the big-city school system, the parents have lost their share in the running of the schools, particularly the low-income parents. Hence the cry for community schools which parents believe would give them more direct involvement in the decisions made for their children. This involvement is vital and parents can add the dimension of understanding their children's needs and interpreting them to teachers. Teachers with this interpretation may recognize the necessity of changing the curriculum, materials, and teaching strategies for inner-city children.

Classroom Conditions and Organization

The presence of a good teacher and the importance of an interesting and stimulating classroom cannot be stressed too much. Children need to feel that the classroom is a place where they will learn and where they are respected as individuals, not rejected because they have problems. What makes a classroom stimulating for inner-city children? Living things—things that grow and can be cared for . . . an animal or plant. The concrete world of the city does not give the child an opportunity to see other forms of life. What a marvel to plant a seed and watch it grow. A new, inexperienced teacher thought that planting a garden would be appropriate for a homework assignment and suggested it to her inner-city children. She failed to take a good look at the community around the school; one child actually tried to dig up the sidewalk to comply with the teacher's request.

Interest centers around the room provide a variety of experiences; for example, an easel, paints and brushes for painting. Lack of supplies is frequently expressed as a problem; newspapers or brown paper can be used as effectively as regular art paper. Scraps of material, buttons, almost any stray item can be put together for a collage. A child may collect items from the street to put together for his picture.

A science center where children can perform simple experiments appropriate for their age level can be completed. Once again a lack of materials should not be cited—floating subjects in water or combining soda and vinegar doesn't require expensive or extensive scientific equipment.

A reading and oral-language center is a vital part of the classroom environment. An extensive supply of books at varying levels of difficulty, containing stories related to and expanding upon the child's experiences, are needed. Books children have written and illustrated should be a part of the supply. Puppets as simple as peanut shells with faces, that go on the child's fingers, to more elaborate puppets, can be used for oral expression. A listening center with tapes or records and earphones is an excellent addition to the center if the budget permits. The tapes can contain stories the teacher has read into the recorder or language-learning experiences for the children to complete; for example, begin stories and permit the children to develop the ending.[10] Also, the child should have an opportunity to record his voice in reading a story, telling it or putting on a play. A group of inner-city children increased their desire to read and discuss stories after the introduction of a tape recorder for their use.

A math center filled with concrete items for counting and manipulating is another necessity. Once again the items can be inexpensive—bottle caps, etc. More elaborate blocks and geometric shapes for puzzles and manipulation would be worthwhile.

Bulletin board displays and pictures should be of people and places within the community to permit the children to identify school with the outside world. Pictures should be predominately of the race or minority group within the classroom. Don't make the mistake of a white teacher who used all white children's pictures when working with a totally black classroom. Whether the pictures should depict the most extreme poverty conditions in the community is left to the decision of the teacher, based on the age and emotional maturity of the children. Obviously the teacher does not want to display only those pictures that are unrealistic or without the child's environmental experiences, as the suburban home with a large lawn and flower garden. Equally as unsatisfactory would be to display just the poverty homes without providing some contrast.

There should be a center for games and puzzles or these should

---

[10]Dorothy J. Skeel, *Developing Creative Ability* (South Holland, Ill.: H. Wilson Corp., 1967).

be placed with the related subject area center—if possible, a relia table with items from other countries under study. However, these should not be placed in the room if the children are not permitted to handle them. Maps and globes to show where the child lives and to show where other people live in the world should be available.

Care should be exercised by the teacher to avoid making the room appear cluttered and overstimulating to the child. Also, the child should have a specific place designated for him in the classroom. Each one should have a share in the responsibility of the upkeep of the room. Items should be put away when children are finished with them. Each child should be responsible to keep the room in order; some teachers prefer to have individual children designated for specific tasks.

Seating arrangements within the classroom are important and the best plan selected should be based on the age and social maturity of the children. Vociferous children should not be placed with seats facing one another—they are simply not conditioned to work that way. However, the arrangement should be relatively informal and always moveable. Children should not be singled out to sit off away from other children, but hyperactive children can be removed to interest centers when the need arises. However, this should not be used as a punishment.

ORGANIZATIONAL PATTERNS

How the class will be organized is an important consideration. Team teaching has been used successfully with inner-city children.[11] A faculty team comprised of a team leader, four teachers (each with a class), a college intern and a team mother provides more individualized instruction, increased motivation for learning, different teaching styles and flexibility in scheduling. Inner-city children need the opportunity provided by the team to identify with many adults. Discipline is maintained more readily and neophyte teachers are more effectively introduced to working with inner-city children in a team-teaching situation.

Organization based on nongraded, continuous progress is beneficial because it removes the failure complex and emphasizes individualization

---

[11]Helen K. MacKintosh, Lillian Gore, and Gertrude Lewis, *Educating Children In The Middle Grades* (Washington, D.C.: U.S. Department of Health, Education, and Welfare, Office of Education, 1965), p. 39.

of instruction. Children are grouped by ages; they begin working at their respective levels, and they move ahead as rapidly as possible. Interest grouping across class or grade lines provides increased motivation because children are encouraged to select their own group based on their interest in a topic. Within-class grouping, organized according to specific skills or friendship groups, adds to both the interest and flexibility of the program. Children can learn to work more effectively with others, and they can move freely from group to group.

ROLE OF THE CHILD IN THE CLASSROOM

Teachers need to guide children toward an understanding of their roles as learners. Frequently this has not been accomplished by the home environment. Parents of inner-city children are often more concerned with the practical consideration of school—can the child get a job, rather than the intellectual side of education. The child must first be motivated to learn. By showing he expects the child to be successful, the teacher assists him in building a good self-concept. As the child gains confidence, he becomes less dependent on the teacher. As he becomes involved in learning activities, his interest increases. The child gradually begins to realize that there are things he wants to learn.

The environment should be more structured in the beginning in order that the child may learn the advantages of organized behavior. Freedom of decisions and choices can be permitted as he learns self-discipline. Initially experiences offered these children should be vital and motivational. They should build upon the children's present background. First the children should be reintroduced to their immediate environment and helped to understand it. Then their horizons should be expanded to a broader environment that they should be helped to understand. Have the children ever been on a bus, gone to the supermarket, visited a museum, baked cookies, had someone really listen while they talked or experienced approval upon completion of a task?

Language Arts Program

DEVELOPING ORAL AND WRITTEN EXPRESSION

What happens to a child who is black, Oriental, or Puerto Rican when all the books he sees in school are about white people? What does this tell a child? Does the child begin to think that his race isn't good enough to be in books or does he wish he were another race? How does he react? Some children become belligerent and try to show everyone who they are, while others will acquiesce and retreat into docility. Others living in a home where they receive love and emotional security can still develop a good self-concept. White children from low socioeconomic homes face similar feelings when they are constantly exposed to middle-class values. They shun the dirt and smell of poverty and assume there is little that is good around them and within themselves. There are other cues in our society that produce the same message—magazines, television, billboards and the people who are holders of important positions. This picture is slowly changing; however, the inclusion of black, yellow and red faces in the reading book is not sufficient without a change in attitude of the people who touch the lives of these children—teachers, principals, social workers, aides. One of the blocks to learning for these children is a poor self-concept. This should be constantly considered as learning experiences are planned for inner-city children.

Inner-city children have been labeled "culturally deprived" or "culturally disadvantaged," but obviously these are poor terms. The inner-city is immersed in a culture—a culture that may be different from middle-class America. As a result of that culture being different from what is generally expected of the child in school, Bereiter and Engelmann "claim disadvantaged children do not have enough time to participate in the same experiences as privileged children. Therefore, selection and exclusion of experiences is necessary to provide those activities which will produce a faster than normal rate of progress."[12] Their discussion is primarily aimed at a preschool program; however, it certainly should be considered when planning programs at any level.

Cultural deprivation is synonymous with language deprivation. It is apparent the disadvantaged child has mastered a language "that is adequate for maintaining social relationships and for meeting his social and material needs, but he does not learn how to use language for obtaining and transmitting information for monitoring his own behavior, and for carrying on verbal reasoning."[13] The disadvantaged child cannot use language "to explain, to describe, to instruct, to inquire, to hypothesize, to analyze, to compare, to deduce and to test."[14] These claims are generalized and rather broad and inclusive. Undoubtedly, it is true that these children have difficulty with the language of the school. However have most schools provided the proper language (particularly oral) experiences for these children?

Keeping these two basic problems in mind (poor self-concept and poor language facility) let's observe the actual dialogue of a teacher and a group of third-graders in the inner-city. The teacher develops an oral language activity with them. This language activity is combined with a social studies concept—poverty. The teacher has a picture of a little girl in ragged clothes who looks rather sad and pathetic. The teacher has three goals: to increase the children's speaking skill, to increase thinking skills through several levels of questioning, to help children realize that there are others who live in poverty.

This is the first time the pupils have worked with the teacher in this way and the responses are not as reflective as was anticipated.

---

[12]Carl Bereiter and Siegfried Engelmann, *Teaching Disadvantaged Children in the Preschool* (Englewood Cliffs, N.J.: Prentice-Hall, Inc., 1966), pp. 6–19.
[13]Bereiter and Engelmann, *Teaching Disadvantaged Children in the Preschool*, p. 42.
[14]Bereiter and Engelmann, *Teaching Disadvantaged Children in the Preschool*, p. 31.

T: I want you to look very carefully at this picture that I have and tell me what you can about the little girl just by looking at the picture. If you will move back I will put it around so that you can all see it.

(This is a concrete question
that allows any child to answer)

P: She is standing up.

P: She is playing with something. She is looking at us.

T: That's right, she is. She is looking right out at us. What else can you tell me about her?

P: She is playing with something.

P: She has bare feet.

P: She is playing with mud. I don't like to play with mud.

T: What else can you tell me? What kind of an expression does she have on her face?

(Children need more direction)

P: Happy.

P: Sad.

T: What else can you tell me about her?

P: She has a polkadot dress on. She is by herself.

T: Right. That is good.

P: She has a bucket of water.

T: Looks that way, doesn't it?

(The teacher now changes and
suggests the children ask her
questions for information)

T: Now would you like to ask me some questions about her so you can learn more about her?

P: Does she not got no arm?

T: She does. You can't see it.

P: Looks like she's cold.

T: Why don't you ask me some questions about her? What would you like to know about her?

P: Is she rich or poor?

P: I think maybe she is poor, that is why she ran away.

T: It looks like she ran away. What makes you think she ran away?

P: It looks like she don't got any parents.

P: It looks like she is on the street. It looks like she is poor. It looks like she don't got no father or mother.

T: Now ask me some questions and I will tell you something about
her.

P: She could have gotten lost or something.

P: She probably be waiting for somebody. They could of didn't wanted
her any more or she is outside playing or she is waiting for her
friend.

T: You have done very well. But how can you find out something
about this little girl? How can you find out? Ask questions, all
right, now what do you want to know?

> (The children have difficulty
> asking questions for informa-
> tion—this may be a result of
> their environment, where fre-
> quently they do not receive
> answers to their questions).

P: What is her name and you ask her what is her address. What is
her house number?

T: You haven't even asked me what country. Maybe she doesn't even
live here in this country.

P: Does she live in Mexico? In England?

T: No. Ask some questions about her.

P: She looks like she is Mexican.

T: How are you going to find out these thing?

P: We can look on the map . . .

T: How are you going to find out about this little girl? The first person,
who wants to ask a question?

P: Me. Where did she come from?

T: She came from a country that is a long, long distance away from
here. She came from India. This is where she was when her picture
was taken.

P: I thought she came from Mexico.

T: What else do you want to ask about her?

P: Is she your friend?

T: Yes, now she is my friend.

P: Has she any parents?

T: She has a mother but she doesn't have any father.

P: Probably he died in the war. Does she have brothers and sisters?

T: Oh yes, she has brothers and sisters, about four or five.

P: You have been there?

T: No, I have never been there.

P: Then how do you know?

T: Because I learned all about this little girl.

P: Is she rich or poor?

T: She is very very poor. In fact in this picture she is starving. Do you know what that means?

P: She doesn't have any food.

P: She eats mud.

T: What else do you want to ask?

P: How is she your friend when she don't even know you?

P: Has she got a doll?

T: Well, you see there are ways that you can help people without even knowing them.

P: There is some junky stuff in this yard and this lady took it and she sells it and takes those rich guys and they give it to the poor.

> (Child is thinking about a
> neighbor who helps other people)

P: Does she take some dogfood and eat it?

T: The dogfood over there is very, very limited. In other words, it is not like buying it out of a can. The dogs get whatever there is left around.

P: Does she have an apple tree?

T: No, she doesn't have an apple tree.

P: She could eat a piece of a squirrel.

T: There are no squirrels in her country. Are there any other questions that you want to ask about her?

P: Does she got a bed? Then how do they sleep?

P: Do they sleep on the floor?

P: Some people sleep on the street.

T: No, they really don't have a house as we think of a house where you can go inside. It is kind of built just out of leftovers.

P: They don't got any water either?

T: Yes, some water. Not running water like you think of it. They have public wells. Anything else?

P: Do they have a swing set or something to play with?

P: They don't have a swing set in the olden days.

T: It is today. It is not those days as you are thinking of a long time ago. It is right now. In fact she is living—she is about four years old.

P: Do they have schools over there?

T: Yes, they do have schools. She doesn't go to school. Do you have any other questions? . . . I want to ask you a couple of questions.

P: What kind hair does she have?

> (Child wants to know something personal about the child. He is saying, "Is she like me?")

P: The same kind of hair that we have.

P: Except that they don't comb it because they don't have a comb.

P: Does she got that much hair like she is out there right now?

P: She has big eyes.

P: Do they got doctors over there?

P: Yes.

T: Suppose we think a little bit about this girl. I told you that she doesn't have any food. She doesn't really have a home to live in. How do you suppose people could help this little girl?

P: Send them some food and money.

P: Do other people not have food?

T: There are a lot of people in this country who don't have food. In India, where this little girl lives. Why do you suppose they don't have any?

P: Because they can't afford any.

P: They have to take their bucket and go hunting and fishing.

P: Do they have any fishing poles?

T: I don't imagine she has one, no. Some of their rivers over there are so spoiled by garbage and things that you put into it that they can't eat the fish.

P: Do they got any snakes out there? Do they have garter snakes?

T: The little green snakes like you think of?

P: No, little black ones.

P: She needs food and clothes.

P: She needs someone to take care of her.

T: That is right. She needs someone to take care of her.

P: Who told you that she had that many brothers and sisters?

The important thing to assess in this experience is the goals:

(1) Did the children participate actively in the discussion developing oral language? Yes. What oral language? Expressing ideas so that others may understand, and contributing to a discussion. Notice that the teacher accepted every contribution of the children.

(2) Did the children extend their thinking skills? Yes. What skills? Moving from one level of thought (concrete) to higher levels of thought (abstract). Also the thoughts included both cognitive (thinking) and affective (feeling) experiences.

(3) Did the children relate to the child in the picture and realize that other people live in poverty? Yes. Obvious in the type of questions they asked.

The teacher did not try to pull thoughts together at the end and have the children draw conclusions from the experience, since they were not ready for it. Nor did the teacher attempt to have the children gain specific knowledge from this activity.

Through this simple activity, these children became active learners. Why? Because they related to the child in the picture and it was within the realm of their experiences.

Realizing that these children had difficulty asking questions for information, the teacher planned an activity that would encourage question asking. She prepared a wrapped package with an article inside. The children were presented with the task of asking questions to find out what was in the box.

T: There is something in this box . . .

P: Can I feel it?

T: No. You have to try and figure out what is in this box by asking questions. You can't say is it this? Is it that? You have to ask questions that will help you figure out what is in the box. The only kind of question that you can ask me would be the kind that I can answer you with yes or no. Now here is a sample of the kind of question that you could ask. You could say, Is it made of wood? And I would say yes or no.

P: Is that little girl in there?

(Remembering the first discussion)

T: No. Now remember that I said you have to ask the kind of questions that I can answer yes or no and you have to work toward finding out what is in the box.

P: Is it made out of wood? Is it made out of steel?

T: No.
P: Is it made out of rubber?
T: I will have to take back what I said. It is partly made out of wood.
P: Is it plastic?
T: No.
P: Does it have legs?
T: No.
P: Does it have wheels?
T: No.
P: Does it have a face?
T: No.
P: It's a picture and it is made out of paper.
T: No.
P: Is it a box?
P: Is it made out of leather?
T: No.
P: Is it a piece of fish?
P: Is it a doll?
T: No.
P: Is it made out of glass?
P: Is it red, white and blue?
T: Part of it is red.
P: Is it black, green, purple?
T: No. Part of it is purple.
P: Purple donkey.
P: Is it a little dress?
T: No.
P: Is it some animal?
T: Yes.
P: It is different colors?
T: Yes.
P: Is it a painting she made for you?
P: We can't guess it.
T: Keep asking questions. You are asking is it this or is it that. Why don't you find out something about it?
P: How can we?
T: By asking questions.
P: Will you tell us one thing about it?

T: If you ask a couple of questions, I will let you shake the box.

P: Is it a house?

T: You are not asking questions about it. What do you know so far about it?

P: That it is a different color and that it is made of colors.

T: It is part wood. That is right.

P: Is it the face of her?

T: No, it doesn't have anything to do with the little girl.

P: Is it a pitcher?

P: Is it a little bucket?

T: No. It doesn't have anything to do with the little girl. What do you know so far about it?

P: That it is different colors and it is part wood.

P: Where did you get it from?

T: It has to be a question that I can answer yes or no.

P: Can we shake it?

T: You can shake it but not too hard.

P: Is it a block?

T: No.

P: Is it puzzles?

T: No.

P: Is it cookies?

T: No.

P: Is it hammers and things?

P: Are you going to open it?

T: You are going to try and find out without my opening it.

P: Is it wooden blocks?

T: Remember I said it was only partly wood. What other kinds of questions can you ask about it to try and find out?

P: May I see what it is?

T: No. Ask some questions about it. We said it wasn't steel.

P: Is there any green in it?

P: Is there yellow?

T: Yes.

P: Do you know what it is?

T: Sure, I put it in there.

P: She got it from her house.

T: I said there was some red in it.

P: Some play apples, play bananas and play grapes.

P: Different-colored rocks?

T: No.

P: What they eat out of.

P: OK, open it then.

T: You haven't asked good questions.

P: It is a statue.

P: You got it from home, what can it be?

T: What are you doing? Instead of asking questions about it, you are guessing. So think of some questions you can ask about it.

P: I don't never know any.

T: Can't think of any questions?

P: Nope. Not one single one.

P: What can you use it for?

P: Can you make a house with it?

T: What are some questions you can ask about what you can do with it?

P: Is it big?

T: Now, Lonnie is getting to some good questions. No, Lonnie, it is not.

P: Is it little? Is it middle-sized?

T: It is a little larger . . .

P: Is it large?

T: No.

P: Is it soft?

T: No. That is a good question. So if it isn't soft—

P: It is hard.

P: Is it hairy?

T: No. Your questions are very good.

P: What kind of wood is it made out of?

P: A wood that is different colors and not the kind of wood that we have.

T: No, it is not pretty wood necessarily. Kind of plain wood.

P: Is it made out of skin?

T: Can you think of any more questions? Now what do you know about it so far?

P: It is different colors and it is hard.

P: It is middle-sized.

T: Very good. How can you find out what we do with it?
P: What they work with, what they eat on.
P: What their floor is made of.
T: I told you it didn't have anything to do with the little girl. You want to find out what you do with it. How would you find out what you do with it? What questions would you ask?
P: Does it take batteries—a motorcar?
P: Do they play with it?
T: Yes, you might call it that.
P: Is it round?
T: Yes.
P: Little round blocks?
T: The whole thing isn't round but part of it is round.
P: She said is it a scarecrow?
T: No. That is made out of part wood, isn't it? There is one thing that you haven't asked me about it.
P: Can you burn it?
T: No. The wood part of it you can burn but you wouldn't want to.
P: Could it be a clock? Is it striped?
T: There is one question you haven't asked me. You haven't asked me if you could eat it.
P: They are food.
P: Is it a sugarcane?
T: No, but it has sugar in it.
P: It is candy.
T: Yes, I'll give each one of you a piece.

From the discussion it is apparent that the children have difficulty using the information they have gathered and piecing it together. Their thought patterns are not well organized. However, as they were given subsequent opportunities to participate in this type of activity, their thought patterns became more organized. They did increase their language facility and did become actively involved. Once again every child could participate with a certain amount of success.

These are just two examples of the types of oral language experiences that inner-city children should participate in daily. The activities should vary, but follow a sequential development from the concrete to more abstract situation. Small group sessions are more effective since a larger number of children get an opportunity to participate.

Other examples of oral activities:

(1) Discussions before and after field trips
(2) Morning news reports
(3) Discussing books that have been read
(4) Discuss pictures depicting emotions—pictures can provide important stimulus for discussions
(5) Use of puppets where children develop their own dialogue for a story (puppets can be made from paper bags, peanuts, sticks)
(6) Use of the telephone to carry on conversations in the classroom
(7) Presentations of TV and radio programs

It is obvious from the reported dialogue that the children need to increase their listening skills. There are numerous activities that can be developed to increase listening skills, but the following types of activities and techniques have been used with inner-city children.

Those activities with a game format:

(1) This may be played with a small group or the entire class. The teacher gives three simple directions to be followed by a child, such as, " Take your book, hop to the board and write the title of the book on the board." The difficulty of the directions can be increased or decreased as the children improve their listening skills. The directions should be given only once.
(2) The teacher names several words that begin alike, such as *city*, *cellar*, and the child is required to add another word beginning with the same sound. Be sure to keep the initial words within their understanding and related to their environment.
(3) A story with sound effects. Tell a story with *key words* in it. Each key word should have a corresponding sound effect. The story might be about a dog, the fire engine and the fire chief.

Key Word	*Sound*
dog	bark
fire engine	siren sound
fire chief	"fire!"

The class can be divided so that a section is responsible for a key word. The children must listen carefully to the story so they will know when to make their sound effect for the key word.

(4) What's wrong?

The teacher tells a simple story about one of the children in the class, but inserts a sentence that is not related. The children must pick out the sentence:

Jeff came to school this morning.
He was wearing a blue shirt.
The moon is very bright.
The shirt was a present from his grandmother.

Or the teacher can substitute incorrect words:

Tanya is going to the zoo.
She will ride the bus.
The animals live in the mountains.
Animal noises frighten Tanya.
She wants to come to the parade.

(5) Listening for key words.

The teacher reads a short story to the children very slowly. A key word has been indicated for the children to count as the story is read.

(6) Listening and vocabulary development.

The teacher reads appropriate poetry to the children. After the poem has been read, the children will recall the color words, sound words and feeling words which they heard as the poem was being read.

(7) Read a descriptive story to the children. After the story has been told, have them draw pictures illustrating the story.

Most of the above activities will also increase the child's vocabulary, but some other activities for this purpose can be mentioned. Using old magazines or newspapers that can be cut up, the child develops his own picture dictionary. It is important for the magazines to contain pictures of the child's race and activities with which he is familiar. A word dictionary can also be made by cutting the words from magazines; the child either draws a picture of the meaning or writes it out.

Paste short stories from children's literature books on cards. Place several questions on the reverse side:

(1) Make up three questions about the story.

(2) Tell the story in your own words.

(3) Write down the words from the story that were difficult.

(4) Pick out the action words and the descriptive words.

LEARNING TO READ

One of the real stumbling blocks for the inner-city child is his difficulty with reading. Numerous reasons for this difficulty can be cited: lack of books or other reading material in the home, failure of parents to read to the child, lack of readiness activities—such as picture puzzles[15]—provided frequently by middle-class homes, questioning of the child and the previously mentioned language difficulty.

Keeping in mind these and the other problems of the inner-city child—poor self-concept and a lack of enriching experiences—the question is raised, How should inner-city children learn to read? There have been numerous attempts to produce multiethnic materials such as the Bank Street Readers, Detroit Public Schools and many of the basal reading series. New alphabet materials such as UNIFON and ITA have been suggested. Research in reading has concluded that there is no one way to teach reading, although decoding methods rank higher for beginning readers. Therefore, this author contends that an individualized or possibly better-titled personalized approach to reading would prove most effective with inner-city children. This conclusion is based on the following:

(1) Present basal materials do not relate to the language and experimental background of the inner-city child and lack motivation.

(2) These same materials do not enhance the self-concept of the child.

(3) The type and development of the materials are not based on the learning style of these children, which tends to be physically oriented.

(4) The grouping arrangement recommended for use with basal materials is not congruent with the needs of the children—it rein-

---

[15]It has been found that mothers from lower socioeconomic areas use coercion to get tasks completed rather than explanation and presentation of the essential information. Hess and Shipman "Early Blocks to Children's Learning," in Webster, *The Disadvantaged Learner,* p. 281.

forces the failure complex and constantly compares each child's ability to the others.

(5) The personal one-to-one relationship with the teacher in an individualized approach meets the need of the child for adult association and approval.

(6) Individualized materials are selected by the choice of the child, which means he is interested and motivated to a certain extent.

(7) Each child in an individualized approach can progress as rapidly as he is able, therefore increasing the success factor.

How to Begin

The early activities for this reading program are based on the language-experience approach. That means that the stories or reading materials are based on the children's language and experiences. An example: the children have just returned from a trip to the zoo. All children have shared in the same experience and are equally as motivated by it. The teacher begins to talk with the children about the trip—what did they enjoy? Which animals were their favorites? Where do certain animals come from? (Here a globe is used to locate places.) The route they took to the zoo? After the children have had the opportunity to contribute their thoughts on the trip, the teacher then suggests that they write a story about it. As the children dictate the details of their experience, it is recorded on the board or, better, on a large manila tablet so that it may be preserved for future reading. The story might read this way:

Our Trip to the Zoo

We took a bus to the zoo.
We saw big animals and small animals.
Cissy liked the monkeys.
Jeff liked the elephant.
The elephant came from Africa.
So did the monkeys.
We fed the animals peanuts.

When the chart is completed, many other learning activities can be completed. The teacher may have each child copy it or use it for individual or total group reading. Children can take turns reading lines or play a game to see who can find certain words the teacher calls out. The purpose of the activity is to increase the child's sight vocabulary.

Experience charts can be developed for common everyday activities in the classroom as well—an experiment, a visitor, a birthday, a holiday, the weather, a story the teacher reads (written in their own words) and stimulating pictures. Each day or several times a day, not necessarily at the same time or for the same purpose, a chart should be constructed.

Individual children should work with the teacher and develop their own chart or story based on their personal experiences. These may be shared with other children, or, if too personal, kept by the child.

As the children increase their sight vocabulary they begin to select books to read. These books can be read for themselves, read to other classmates and to their teacher. When a child finishes a book, he may wish to draw a picture about it, or select another one to read.

In addition to selecting their books for reading, the children continue to work with the teacher on experience charts for the development of skills and to increase vocabulary. The previously discussed oral-language and listening experiences work in very well with this reading approach.

A *Typical Reading Period*

Each child is reading a book of his choice or completing some activity with his book, such as writing a story or drawing a picture. While the children are busy reading, the teacher will have individual conferences with the children; a child may request a conference or the teacher may ask for one. During the individual conference, the child may relate some incident from the current book he is reading or read a portion he wants the teacher to hear. The teacher may question the child about the book he is reading or prepare some skill activity that the child needs. If more than one child needs the same skill, then the teacher may take these children together as a group. The teacher can vary the length of the conference from five to ten minutes, depending on the needs of the child. Not every child will need an individual conference every day. The teacher will need to keep careful records of each child's progress—his strengths and weaknesses, his interests and activities completed.

Ways to Stimulate Reading

The same type of activities as described are continued through the primary levels, and occasionally a chart will be developed with upper-grade children. Children in the upper-grade levels have gained more facility with reading and can enjoy independent activities with books. If several children have read the same book, a discussion among them can occur, based on questions they have posed:

(1) What did you like about the author's writing?

(2) What was the author trying to say?

(3) How might you have changed the ending of the story?

Another favorite activity of children is to prepare a diorama depicting an important happening in the book or a peep box. Both can be made from shoe boxes and scraps of construction paper, buttons, etc.

Television shows with the scripts prepared from the stories the children have read are fun to produce. There can be elaborate paper costumes or just necessary props. The ending of the story can be omitted to encourage others to read it.

The task of writing or giving an oral book report can quickly turn off a child from reading if he knows it is a requirement when he finishes a book. However, he can fill in the following wheel to keep a record of the books he has read:

As he fills in the triangle the child adds a number, and in a small notebook he keeps the name of the book and author. The teacher may wish to discuss many of the books with the child, not to check whether he has read them, but rather to increase the level of comprehension. Writing letters to the author of the book and discussing the enjoyment of characters is a fun activity for children. Of course, the receipt of a letter in turn from the author increases the motivation to read others. The author recalls a boy who read almost every book of a famous writer of animal books, so he sent off a letter to the author. There were tears in his eyes when he learned the author had died.

Books for Readers

One of the advantages of individualized reading for the inner-city child is the self-selection. The child picks the books he wants to read; however, there must be appropriate books within the classroom or library for his selection. If the child is black, he needs access to books such as *Striped Ice Cream* by Joan Lexau; *The Contender* by Robert Lipsyte; *A Ride on High* by Candida Palmer; *Lillie of Watts: A Birthday Discovery* by Mildred Pitts Walter; *The Soul Brothers and Sister Lou* by Kristin Hunter; all stories are about ghetto children's lives. Also, *Bright April* by Marguerite de Angeli; *Durango Street and Mystery of the Fat Cat* by Frank Bonham; and the delightful collections of poetry, *On City Streets: An Anthology of Poetry* by Nancy Larrick; *The Me Nobody Knows: Children's Voices from the Ghetto* by Stephen M. Joseph; and the not-to-be-forgotten *Bronzeville Boys and Girls* by Gwendolyn Brooks.[16]

Puerto Rican children will relate to *Candita's Choice* by Mina Lewiton, a book that describes the adjustment problems in New York City. *That Bad Carlos* is a story of a boy who is acquiring a bad reputation. Family life is portrayed in *The Spider Plant*.

Mario, by Marion Garthwaite, relates a Mexican-American boy's shock at seeing a modern city. Poverty in Mexico is portrayed in *My Name Is Pablo*.

Depicting poverty for the white child—*Maggie Rose, Her Birthday*

---

[16]Augusta Baker, *Books About Negro Life for Children*, New York Public Library, 20 West 43rd Street, New York, New York, 10019.

Christmas and *A Tree for Peter*. In other countries, poverty is described in Paris, *The Family under the Bridge*.

In addition to the above, the usual collection of good children's books should be provided.

CREATIVE WRITING EXPERIENCES

Acceptance of the child's writing efforts whatever they may be is a prerequisite to the development of creative writing experiences. The teacher who is more concerned about the periods, subject and verb agreement does not encourage young writiers. Adult, seasoned writers don't take kindly to criticism of their writing efforts, so imagine the effect on fledglings. If writing is to be truly creative, then acceptance of the product is necessary. Inner-city children will not be bound by conventions in their language, especially those involved in the language-experience reading approach. One first-grade child (who was learning to read from a basal reader), when asked if he would like to dictate a story to the teacher, began, "This is Sue. Sue is a girl. This is Sue's birthday. She wants a bicycle." When asked who Sue was, the child indicated he didn't know, nor did he understand what he was dictating.

The first writing experience for these children should be very personal and can be stimulated by pictures. Topics such as "I Am Black," "This Is My Neighborhood," "I Wish," "My Family," or " How I Feel About ___" are good. Music appropriate for the age level is also a good stimulus—modern popular music or soul music can be used.

Concrete poetry is a good beginning in poetry for these children. The teacher can bring in objects for the children to feel, such as sandpaper, stones, cloth, wood, metals, animals, and then have them write about their feelings from the experiences.

The ribbon of concrete wound its way through the countryside.

Other early forms of poetry to use are cinquain and haiku. Both of these provide opportunities for every child to be successful.

Cinquain

First line: one word, giving title
Second line: two words, describing title
Third line: three words, expressing an action
Fourth line: four words, expressing a feeling
Fifth line: one word, a synonym for title.[17]

City

Milling people
Traffic moving fast
No where to go
Lonely.

" Haiku is a Japanese verse form consisting of three lines totaling seventeen syllables. It is usually on some subject in nature and has only the necessary words. The first and last lines have five syllables and the second has seven."[18] Here the teacher should beat out the rhythm of the syllables.

The clouds are soft pink
Slowly moving by the door
Sailing to others.

Sounds of their environment produce a stimulus for writing for inner-city children. Records are available with the sounds of the city. These can be played over and over again. Or open the window and use the sounds of the street. These sounds are so familiar and yet the child may never have really listened to them

The most frequent opportunity for writing will come when the child feels the need to express himself about an experience or activity in which he has engaged. Dictating this experience to the teacher or

---

[17]Walter T. Petty and Mary Bowen, *Slithery Snakes and Other Aids to Children's Writing* (New York: Appleton-Century-Crofts, 1967), p. 50.
[18]Ibid., pp. 51–52.

writing it himself will give the child a chance to release his feelings about it. Another type of writing will be that of thank-you notes to other classes, or invitations.

Children should not be forced into writing, but when they meet with approval and success during the initial experiences, they will be more encouraged to try again.

SUMMARY

The importance of the language arts program cannot be stressed enough. Here are found the vital experiences the child needs to express himself orally and in writing, learn more about himself and his world through reading, and communicate to others his feelings and beliefs. An effective, well-rounded language arts program should be the core of the child's school-learning activities.

BIBLIOGRAPHY

Bonham, Frank. *Durango Street.* New York: E. P. Dutton & Co., Inc., 1965.

———. *Mystery of the Fat Cat.* New York: E. P. Dutton & Co., Inc., 1968.

Brooks, Gwendolyn. *Bronzeville Boys and Girls.* New York: Harper & Row, Publishers, 1956.

Carlson, Natalie. *The Family under the Bridge.* New York: Harper & Row, Publishers, 1958.

DeAngeli, Marguerite. *Bright April.* Garden City, N. Y.: Doubleday & Company, Inc., 1946.

Garthwaite, Marion. *Mario, A Mexican Boy's Adventure.* Garden City, N. Y.: Doubleday & Company, Inc., 1960.

Joseph, Stephen. *The Me Nobody Knows, Children's Voices from the Ghetto.* New York: Avon Books, 1969.

Kristin, Hunter. *The Soul Brothers and Sister Lou.* New York: Charles Scribner's Sons, 1968.

Larrick, Nancy. *On City Streets: An Anthology of Poetry.* New York: Bantam Books, Inc., 1968.

Lewiton, Mina. *Candita's Choice.* New York: Harper & Row, Publishers, 1959.

———. *That Bad Carlos.* New York: Harper & Row, Publishers, 1964.

Lexau, Joan M. *Striped Ice Cream*. Philadelphia: J. B. Lippincott Co., 1968.

Lipsyte, Robert. *The Contender*. New York: Harper & Row, Publishers, 1967.

Palmer, Candida. *A Ride on High*. Philadelphia: J. B. Lippincott Co., 1966.

Sawyer, Ruth. *Maggie Rose, Her Birthday Christmas*. New York: Harper & Row, Publishers, 1952.

Sereday, Kate. *A Tree for Peter*. New York: The Viking Press, Inc., 1941.

Sommerfelt, Aimee. *My Name Is Pablo*. New York: Criterion Books, Inc., 1965.

Speevack, Yetta. *The Spider Plant*. New York: Atheneum Publishers, 1965.

Walter, Mildred Pitts. *Lillie of Watts: A Birthday Discovery*. Los Angeles: The Ward Richie Press, 1969.

Social Studies

OBJECTIVES

Social studies objectives for the inner-city child are formulated with consideration for his learning problems and environmental factors. Broad general objectives include:

Acquire Knowledge:
> Of the history of minority groups and their contributions to the cultural heritage of the nation.

> Of the child's immediate environment to enable him to understand its relationship to the larger world.

> Of the democratic process and the importance of the individual assuming his responsibility.

Acquire an understanding:

> Of the contribution that each individual makes to the group of which he is a member.

> Of the reasons why prejudice occurs and its effect on society and the relationships of people.

> Of the problems of poverty and prejudice that occur in other cultures of the world.

Of the relationship of what is learned in school to the child's everyday
   activities.

To develop an attitude:

Of the worth of each individual as a member of society.

Of the value of learning and its potential to provide a better future
   for each child.

Develop skill:

In communicating with others through oral and written methods.

In getting along with others in the immediate group and in society.

In acquiring information through critical reading, listening and observing.

In inquiry and problem solving.

These objectives vary in accordance with the specific needs and
background of the group. The emphasis here is placed on the necessity
for experiences in social studies to compensate for the disadvantages
the child brings to school with him.

Obviously, most of the problems the inner-city child faces as he
enters school are the result of deprivation in his early formative years.
His future appears quite different to him than it does to the average
child. He sees little offered by the traditional school that applies to
his life. Therefore, teachers must adapt their programs to meet the
needs and interests of these children. Social studies is an important
area. What adaptations are necessary?

SELECTION OF CONTENT

There are certain factors inherent in the social studies that are
not as problematic in other subject areas. Webster relates the following:
"the content in social studies is of highly verbal nature—more reading
is required than in almost any other subject; topics are frequently removed from realities of life chronologically and spatially; and many
of the values, attitudes, and behaviors advocated are contrary to those
of the disadvantaged."[19] Also the materials available portray experiences
that are often remote from the lives of the inner-city child. An awareness

---

[19]Webster, *The Disadvantaged Learner*, p. 586.

of these factors will permit teachers to compensate for them. Considering these children's learning problems as well as the problems inherent in the social studies, what should be included in the content of the social studies program?

The goal of such a program is for the child to learn the same basic concepts of social studies as any elementary school child; however, adaptation will be necessary to relate the content to their everyday lives. The following model serves as a basis for planning programs for the urban child.

IMMEDIATE ENVIRONMENT   REMOVED ENVIRONMENT

Kindergarten—Grade 1

The child as a person and his feelings. The child as he relates to groups. *His* home, family and school—discussion centers on the type of family relationships that occur in the environment of the child; an example might be the presence of different adults in the home such as aunts, uncles, grandmothers, etc., or the absence of a father. No attempt should be made to place emphasis on the typical mother-father-child relationship of the middle-class home. To develop the self-concept, stress should be placed on the individual and his role.

Local community—stress available libraries, museums, parks, recreation areas and community services.

Important people—discuss leaders in the community and nation but, most important, select leaders from the children's culture such as Martin Luther King for Negro children.

Select a culture that has a similar family relationship—for example, have the Mexican-American learn Mexican customs.

Grade 2

Democratic processes—discuss the problems of a minority using those apparent within the classroom; for ex-

Group minority problems in national relationship.

Grade 2 (continued)

ample, the failure to choose a favorite game or the presence of more girls than boys.

National heritage—stress contributions of their particular culture in areas such as music, art.

Symbols such as flag, holidays, freedom.

Economic concepts—work in the family, neighborhood, school. Study problems of lack of money, resources, unemployment.

Other areas of the nation with similar problems.

Grade 3

Historical—choose a local memorial, monument, or early settlement of the area.

Early pioneers, Indians, people who came from lands specific to the group's ancestry.

Relationships of urban and rural areas—children learn about the contributions of the rural area to cities in terms of food, labor, purchases; children in the city learn of their contributions to the country.

Cities or rural areas beyond local environment.

Communication—within the classroom use methods beyond spoken language, e.g., facial expressions, actions.

Systems including different languages relating to their cultural background.

Transportation—stress modes used in their community and the problems presented.

Link to the previous study of cities and their available modes of transportation.

Grade 4

Geographic concepts of locale—study climate, rainfall and terrain.

Similar geographic conditions in other areas of the world.

Contrasting geographic conditions existing in close proximity to the local environment and in other parts of the world.

Social, economic and political problems of the community.

National and world problems of a similar nature.

Grade 5

Governmental processes—begin with class organization, school and community.	State and national government—in relation to early development; birth of the nation.
	Contrasting governments.
Local racial or nationality problems.	Discuss the Civil War, Spanish-American War, etc, to help the children understand the possible origins of their problems.

Grade 6

Family background of children in classroom.	Nations of children's ancestors.
Neighboring community's ancestral background.	United Nations.

This model does not provide an exhaustive list of the content to be included in the social studies, nor are the grade lines intended to be restrictive. The model attempts to show a pattern of relationships between the concerns of the immediate environment and the removed environment. This model stresses the necessity of beginning with the here and now and expanding to that which is distant and past.

SPECIAL INSTRUCTIONAL CONSIDERATIONS

Adaptation of the content is important, but it is not sufficient to allow the inner-city learner to receive maximum benefit from the instruction. Other necessary considerations involve teaching methods, activities and materials.[20]

Teaching Methods

Special teaching methods are required for these children to compensate for their inadequacies in school. The following pertinent methods are found to be effective:

---

[20]MacKintosh, Gore, and Lewis, *Educating Children in the Middle Grades*, p. 39.

The provision of cues which are salient and concrete, the ensuring
of direct participation in the learning situation by every child, and
the reinforcement of correct or desired responses . . .[21]

Teachers must adapt teaching methods to avoid pursuing abstractions without providing concrete examples. It is important for teachers
to move from the concrete to the abstract.

The teacher should use open-ended questioning to motivate thinking and to remove the block of the one-right-answer syndrome. Repeti-
tive use of this method is necessary because first experiences may be
discouraging.

An example of the type of open-ended inquiry that should be used
with inner-city children to help them understand their problems is
portrayed by the following dialogue. There has been an argument between two children in the group. The teacher pursues the causes of
the argument with the children:

T: What was the fight about?
P: About Tanya and him shooting each other.
T: Why do you suppose he pulled the chair out from under Tanya?
P: Because Tanya was hitting him.
T: Why was she hitting him?
P: Because he was bothering her. She was bothering me.
T: Why was she bothering you?
P: Because I didn't let her use my Footsie.

(A toy attached to the foot
for jumping)

T: So what seems to be the trouble between the two of them? What
was the problem?
P: That Michael—
T: What was really the problem?
P: He could of told on her.
T: Now stop and think about it. What was really the trouble? What
do you think the real problem was?
P: That I didn't let her use my Footsie.
T: In other words, she wanted something that you had. So what really
was the problem then? What do you think it is? Yes, he wouldn't

[21]Sophia Bloom, "Improving the Education of Culturally Deprived Children: Applying
Learning Theory to Classroom Instruction," *Chicago School Journal* XLV (December,
1963), 126–31.

share with her. Can you think then what might have been a different way to behave?

P: Everything would have been all right—if he hadn't pulled the chair from under her.

T: You think that if they had shared, everything would have been all right. Tanya and Michael, will you show us how it would have been if you had shared? Show us what would have happened if you would shared.

(The children role-play the
sharing process)

T: All right, what makes the difference here?

P: He shared with her so no fight would start.

T: Why do you suppose people behave the way they do? Who do you suppose—

P: 'Cause they don't want to get in trouble.

T: Stop and think a moment, Tanya, why is it that people don't want to share? Or why is it that they behave the way they do?

P: Because they don't like the other people. Sometime they are spoiled.

T: What do you mean by spoiled?

P: They always want their way.

T: Anyone else?

P: They aren't bothering other people. But Tanya asked Michael for a Footsie and then they ask someone else and they say no. Like if they ask someone else and they say yes, they are a nice guy.

P: Like if Tanya had Footsie and Michael asked for it and Tanya wouldn't let him, so if Michael had a Footsie—

P: If Lanie and Robert had a Footsie and Lanie asked Robert could he use his Footsie and Robert went home and Lanie came back with his Footsie, Robert asked him and Lanie said no.

(The teacher switches to
another incident that had
occurred in the hall)

T: Now something happened out in the hall while these children were out there—you tell us what happened.

P: There was a boy out in the hall and his name was Brian and he was looking at us while we were playing our play and then Jeffrey went over there and pushed him.

T: All right now, why did Jeffrey push him?

P: 'Cause he was nosey. Because he was waiting for somebody and Jeffrey didn't know it.

T: Why did he push him, Tanya?

P: Because he was going to tell everybody else.

P: He could have been meddling, picking at him and stuff.

T: You boys aren't thinking carefully. Now think about it. Why do you suppose—here we are out in the hall and Brian is not really a part of our group you see out there. He was just standing there; now what did Jeff really do when he went over and pushed him?

P: Meddling—

T: No, I think you are using a word you don't really know. What do you mean by meddling?

P: Picking on him.

T: He wasn't picking on him.

P: They don't know. They weren't even out there.

T: That doesn't make any difference. Don't you think they can tell just by thinking about it? Why do you suppose—now picture us out there in the hall. Here we are, the four of us, talking and kind of standing over there in the corner and the boys here think, He is listening to our conversation, and what we are doing, and so Jeff goes over and pushes him. Why do you suppose he went over and pushed him? What was he saying to Brian by pushing him?

P: To get out of here.

T: Why do you suppose he wanted him to get out of here?

P: So he couldn't listen.

P: Now can I tell the rest? He was waiting for somebody—

T: Wait a moment, before you tell us that—

P: Jeffrey didn't know he was waiting there for somebody and then Jeffrey pushed him.

T: We still haven't really answered why he pushed him.

P: I know, I know. Because Jeffrey didn't know Brian was waiting for the lady and the girl.

T: This is very true. But don't you think there is some real reason behind it?

P: Brian might tell somebody or something.

T: Do you think that he was worried about Brian telling someone? What do you think was his real reason for pushing him?

P: He didn't want nobody to know about it.

T: All right. Here we were, a small group, and he didn't want him to get into the group, did he? Can you think of other times when people do this?

P: When they don't want nobody to listen in their conversation.

T: Is it only listening in their conversation? What are some other times when you don't want someone to get into some activity or something that you are doing?

P: Because they are disturbing you.

T: Do you think it was because they are disturbing you? What is another reason?

P: They are supposed to be in a classroom and they might be tardy. They might be tardy and we don't want them to get in trouble.

P: They would get a bad report on their report card.

T: All right, can you tell me what would have been a different way that he could have acted toward Brian? What could he have done?

P: He could have said, "Why are you waiting out in the hall when you should have been in the room?"

T: All right, he could have said to him, "Why are you waiting out in the hall?" All right, what else could he have done?

P: I could have said, "What are you doing out there, Brian?" He could have said, "I am waiting for somebody." I could have said, "Ain't you going to go in the room," and then he would say No, he was waiting for somebody there.

T: Think of another thing—

P: That is a good way to start a fight.

T: So what might have happened?

P: They might have had a fight in the hall and get a paddle from Mr. Gregory.

P: Jeffrey could have said, "You are going to be tardy."

T: All right, that is another thing he could have done.

P: I know another one. He was getting kind of cold as he was soaking wet.

T: That is true. Brian was wet. Now what would you say would have been the best way for him to behave?

P: Just go over there and ask him why he was waiting in the hall. And Brian could have told him and Jeffrey would have walked back and sat down and started listening what you are saying.

T: That is right. So why do you suppose people behave the way they do?

P: Because they don't want other people to listen in their conversation and they don't want a fight to start.

P: And they don't want other people—they want other people to mind their own business.

The main difficulty for the children in this discussion was the ability to concentrate for any length of time and to stick to the line of questioning. However, they have sophisticated insight (possibly more than the middle-class child) into their own and others' behavior. The use of this same approach numerous times will lead to improved concentration by the children and they will be better able to follow the questioning. In this activity, the children were participating in inquiry; they identified a problem (group behavior problem), suggested hypotheses (other ways to behave to avoid the problem), tested out their ideas and arrived at some generalizations (they think most want people to mind their own business). By beginning the inquiry process with a problem that is a part of their daily experiences, the teacher is able to motivate more active participation on the part of most children in the class. Everyone has had the experience of an argument and can contribute to the discussion. This activity then leads to the presentation of a problem that is abstract, out of their immediate environment, a community problem—"Why can't people agree on a location for the new school?" or "Why is there pollution in our city or local community?"

To relate the activities of school to the children's outside world is important. Therefore current affairs and controversial issues must be a part of the instruction. Children soon realize that what they are learning aids them in solving their daily problems and provides understanding of others' problems. They soon realize that history is happening right now and that there is a relationship between past history and current events.

CURRENT AFFAIRS

When to Start

As soon as children come to school, they should be introduced to the current events within their understanding. Teachers can start with reports of events in the children's lives as an introduction. The first concept to be learned is that events make news. The next step is to learn what news is important. Many teachers start the day with the development of a class newspaper containing items from the children's lives. After the children have developed an understanding of what a newspaper should contain, items are included from other rooms in the school, the community, nation and world. An example of what such a newspaper might contain follows:

Today is October 24, 19—
The weather is warm and sunny.
Sharon Gray's house burned last night.
It is located at 24 Locust Street.
Shadyside School will hold an Ice
Cream Social.
It will be Wednesday at 8:00 in the
evening.
The Riverside Community Park will
build a swimming pool.
Boys and girls can learn to swim.
National elections will be held next
month.
Our parents will elect a President of
the United States.

Some variations of this activity are: Small groups of children might prepare their own newspaper or draw pictures of current events and discuss them with the class. Teachers can clip pictures from newspapers and magazines and discuss them with the children, who can then develop captions that demonstrate their understanding of the events in the pictures. These pictures also provide display material for the bulletin board.

To provide children with a thorough understanding of events of importance occurring locally, nationally or in the world, the teacher should plan problem-solving situations or units of study. Examples of such events might be a natural catastrophe such as a flood, tornado or hurricane; political campaigns; space events; wars and confrontations; and events that relate to past or current topics of study.

Continuation throughout the elementary-school grades of these and other activities concerning current events will foster favorable attitudes toward and natural concern about affairs of the world. The enthusiasm and interest displayed by the teacher are vital factors in the success of these activities.

Suggested Activities

Bulletin Boards

A bulletin board should be reserved for displaying news items or pictures relating to current affairs. An important point to remember is the necessity for frequent changing of its contents. Captions on the board such as "What's New?" "What in the World is Going On?" "News of Our World" stimulate interest.

Division of the board into areas for local, state, national and international items helps children differentiate the news events. The use of a world map on the board enables children to locate the area of the news event and helps them develop map skills. A thread of yarn attached to the location of the event and leading to the written report helps the children associate the place and the event. Responsibility for the bulletin board can be assigned to committees of children or be a dual obligation of the teacher and children.

News Reporting

A variety of organizational patterns can be used to assign children the responsibility of reporting the news. For example, a child might be assigned the responsibility for the news of one day or one week, or committees of children can be assigned the responsibility for a certain period of time. Tape recording of these reports provides some variety.

The establishment of a mock radio or TV station within the classroom supplies more reality for the news-reporting situation. Special broadcasts or programs can be planned when outstanding events take place. Some classrooms may wish to conduct a daily morning-news broadcast with reporters assigned specific areas of the news. Intermediate-grade children may provide the news program for the entire school over the public-address system. Included in these programs may be school news of interest to all.

Items for children to remember when reporting the news:

(1) Do I understand what is happening in the news events?

(2) Can I discuss it with the other children?

(3) Do I know enough about it to answer most of the questions the children might ask?

(4) Are there any words that I'll need some help in pronouncing?

(5) Is the event of interest to most of the children, or will it add knowledge to a topic we are studying?

Class Newspaper

The organization of the class into a newspaper staff to publish and distribute a school newspaper provides realistic experience for news reporting. Reporters can be assigned to secure news of the different classes, the school office and special events. Additional reporters can use outside sources to obtain significant local and national news. Many language skills, as well as social skills, are developed by interviewing people and writing news reports.

Role-Playing, Discussion and Debates

Role-playing can be used to advantage with news events. Role-playing is regarded as most effective with the inner-city children.[22] It requires that children have a thorough understanding of the event before they attempt to act out the situation for others. Dramatizing a summit meeting or the speech of a famous person helps children realize what the event was like.

Discussions can be organized in many ways. The entire class might research a specific topic and attempt to present different points of view, or a news program might be watched on TV (either at school or at home) and discussed. When differences of opinion occur within the group, a debate provides a valuable experience. Both sides can present their views and the children in the class can decide which side presents the best argument. Before the debate takes place, ground rules must be established for time limits on speaking, the use of notes and the manner of answering the opposition.

---

[22]Fannie R. Shaftel and George Shaftel, *Role-Playing for Social Values: Decision Making in the Social Studies* (Englewood Cliffs, N.J.: Prentice-Hall, Inc., 1967), p. 149.

Reading Newspapers

The presence of a daily newspaper in the classroom or library is excellent stimulation for developing the habit of reading newspapers. It is also advisable to secure several popular news magazines to complete the resources. Even primary-grade children benefit from the pictures presented.

Mere reading of news material without learning to recognize biased presentations and propaganda techniques is useless. The provision of news materials with differing points of view helps children understand how the same news events can be reported differently if the reporters possess opposing viewpoints.

Controversial Issues

Many a teacher steps lightly for a variety of reasons when issues of controversy arise in the news or classroom. Fear of losing his job, his own prejudice, lack of knowledge of the issue, school policy, community feeling or a lack of concern are possible causes for a teacher's timidity in this area. Controversial issues, from racial problems to the population explosion, are found in almost every newspaper or newscast. How can they be avoided? Should they be avoided?

Certain controversial issues should be discussed with the inner-city child, for he needs the opportunity to study all sides of an issue and to make his own decisions. Teachers should use discretion when selecting issues for study. Several criteria should be applied:

(1) Are the children mature enough to thoroughly understand the issue?

(2) Do the children have sufficient background experiences to critically appraise the issue?

(3) Will the study of the issue help attain the goals of the school and community?

(4) Is the issue of social, political or economic significance?

(5) Will the children become better informed, thoughtful citizens as a result of the study?

The manner in which a teacher approaches the study of controversial issues is of vital importance. The teacher who has a chip on his shoulder about the issue or one who is prejudiced, opinionated or possesses an extreme point of view and teaches only one side of an issue would be wise to avoid the study. A teacher who feels he cannot discuss an issue without showing his prejudice does his children a disservice in attempting the study. One of the main purposes in having children research these issues is to develop in them the habit of approaching an issue with an open mind, securing the facts on all sides and then making a decision if necessary. A prejudiced teacher who permits that prejudice to show defeats this purpose.

Suppose a riot took place in your city last night. Today, depending upon the person reporting the event, it is being given labels such as " racial," " vandalism," " a demonstration against injustice," or " an overthrow of the laws." The children arrive in school very excited about the event and eager to discuss it. What do you do? How do you approach it? Obviously you can't ignore the issue because it is a part of the children's world. Rather than permit the children to tell what they have heard about the riot, the teacher might suggest that they list a series of questions for which they will be required to secure answers.

(1) How did the riot start?
(2) Where did the riot start?
(3) Is it known who was responsible for starting it?
(4) How much damage was done?
(5) Why did the riot begin?
(6) Might it happen again?
(7) What can be done to prevent it from happening again?

Answers to these questions should be found by listening to news reports (in school when possible) presented by several stations, reading papers and talking to several people who were in the area, if this can be arranged. All children should record the answers they secure, give the source, and then compare them the next day when they arrive in school. If it is determined that the riot was caused by some deep-seated community problem, a thorough study of the issue should be undertaken by children in the intermediate grades if school policy permits. Young children should pursue the topic to the depth of their understanding and ability to secure information. Children should interview citizens of the community, assess their feelings about the problem, find out what laws govern the problem and determine whether the laws are being enforced. The teacher should provide opportunity for children to discuss possible solutions to the problem. Children should learn that the true facts involved in this type of situation are often difficult to find. They should assess the validity of the information they secure.

OTHER ACTIVITIES

Working in Committees

The group experiences of the inner-city child prior to his entrance into school are not organized generally for the attainment of specific goals. The ability to get along with others is a skill that should be acquired as early as possible. The child learns the skills of cooperative behavior by sharing playthings; working on projects with other children; and participating in group activities such as singing, dancing and listening to stories. At the kindergarten level, committees should be small, consisting of two or three children; the task should be of a simple nature. Building a house with blocks, getting the milk or cleaning up materials in the play areas are suggested as beginning activities for committee work. Later in kindergarten and in first grade, more formal tasks can be assigned such as preparing a story for creative dramatics, drawing a movie roll of a story or finding answers to questions by looking at pictures. One first-grade class organized a pet show with committees of children responsible for invitations, judging, refreshments, prizes and care of pets. Children soon learn that the success of such an activity is dependent upon each person cooperating and completing his share of the task.

Continual involvement in committee work throughout the elementary grades is necessary to maintain and refine skill in working together. As children mature they are capable of working in larger groups (of perhaps five or six members) and of completing more difficult tasks. It is crucial that the teacher establish a definite purpose for committee work and that the children understand this purpose.

Organization

The method of selecting members for committees can vary depending upon the group of children and the purpose. Classes of children who have few discipline problems and get along well with one another can generally be permitted to select committee memberships of their choice, based on each individual's interest in a particular subject or task. However, classes of children who experience considerable difficulty in getting along, have discipline problems or have too many leaders should be organized in committees by the teacher. At times it is beneficial for the teacher to select particular students for a committee in order to meet individual differences. For example, the child who is exceptional in art may be placed on a committee in which he can use his talent. Or, the child not very adept in research skills should receive help when placed on a committee of children more capable. It is not necessarily good, however, to place outstanding children with the very slow, for too great a discrepancy in ability may result in frustration for all concerned.

The teacher who has never worked with committees before or a class that has not had experience in working in committees may wish to begin the activity one committee at a time. Using this method the teacher organizes one committee to work on a task; at the completion of its responsibility, she organizes another committee. This method allows the teacher more time to work with each group to guide its activities. After all members of the class have participated in this experience, the whole class can be organized into committees.

Teacher-Pupil Planning

Successful committee experiences depend considerably upon the routines established within the classroom. Children respond more favorably when they have the opportunity to aid in developing guidelines for a project.

After discussion with the teacher, the children established the following guidelines:

The chairman should:
(1) Understand the responsibility of his committee
(2) Help each person understand his task
(3) Be sure each person completes his task.
(4) Be accepting of the opinions and suggestions of committee members.

(5) Report the committee's progress and problems concerning materials to the class.

(6) Be sure members share materials.

Committee members should:

(1) Share materials with others.

(2) Listen to the other committee members' and the chairman's suggestions.

(3) Complete their task on time.

(4) Do their share of the work.

(5) Be willing to help others.

The guidelines that have been established by the class should be referred to daily before beginning the work. In addition, when a problem arises, the teacher should suggest that the children analyze the cause of the problem and check the guidelines for a solution. Children become more self-reliant and self-disciplined when they share in the process of making the rules.

Within the framework of committee responsibility, intellectual skills of using reference materials, locating information, outlining and notetaking, critical thinking and making oral and written reports are utilized. Quickly recognized is the ease with which the social studies and the language arts can be interrelated through the development of these skills.

Locating Information

Skills children need for locating information are:

(1) Knowledge of available resources;

(2) Understanding of how the resource is organized—alphabetically, topically, etc;

(3) Ability to use the table of contents, which lists the major headings;

(4) Ability to use the index, which cites a page number for each entry;

(5) Knowledge of cross references, which indicate a related topic that may give additional information;

(6) Ability to glean information from illustrations; and

(7) Ability to read maps, graphs and charts.

Outlining and Note-taking

Information is outlined to provide a skeleton of the important points. An outline is useful in helping a child organize his information; however, useless outlining of page after page of material for practice is a waste of time. Because an outline presents information in a shortened and simplified form giving only the important points about a topic, children should start with the short form. The main points about a topic are called the main topics or main headings and are designated by Roman numerals. Points about the topic that fall under the main headings are subtopics or subheadings and are designated by capital letters. Details about the subtopics follow them and are designated by numbers, as in the following example:

    I. Africa
        A. Geography
            1. Mountains
            2. Rain forests
            3. Rivers

Note-taking necessitates a decision regarding the purpose of the information. Before they start to take notes children should be encouraged to ask themselves:

(1) Am I attempting to entertain someone with the information?
(2) Am I selecting information that I think an audience would not know?
(3) Am I selecting information I think everyone should know about the topic?

After they have answered these questions they can begin to select the appropriate information.

Critical Thinking

Children are encouraged to use a variety of resource materials as they search for information to fulfill their committee tasks. The resource materials should stimulate critical thinking, initiating questions such as: Does the author of the material express a point of view? Does he use any methods of propaganda in his writing? Does the information vary from source to source? Is the author stating fact or opinion?

When the information has been collected and reported to the class, another opportunity for developing thinking skills arises. Analysis of this information is necessary. Did the committee look at all sides of the issue? Did they present the information accurately or did they express their own opinions? The teacher is responsible for directing these questions to the children so that each child will become accustomed to asking them of himself.

Oral and Written Reports

Skills needed for oral and written reports can be developed in the wide variety of activities involved in presenting committee reports to the class. These skills can also be identified as expressive skills, for the children express themselves in writing, speaking or drawing. After research has been completed the development of a method of sharing each committee's information with the group becomes necessary. Criteria for the success of this method are (1) Did the children gain knowledge from the reports? (2) Did they exhibit an interest in the reports? The guidelines established for reporting include:

(1) Present the information in such a way that others will be interested in the topic.
(2) Be sure the information is accurate and easily understood. Don't obscure the information in gimmicks to develop interest.

The type of information that has been secured will, to a certain extent, determine the choice of presentation. Children should learn what type of presentation best communicates the information they have to report. The oral skills to be developed are:

(1) To acquire poise and confidence in a group situation
(2) To speak with expression
(3) To acquire fluency in phrasing
(4) To speak clearly and slowly
(5) To express an idea so that it may be understood
(6) To adjust the volume of voice to the size of the group

Panel Discussions

Organizing information for a panel discussion is generally better accomplished by intermediate-grade children, but variations of the panel can be presented by young children. For example, first- or second-grade committee members can prepare their part of the presentations on charts, with or without pictures they have drawn. If a child has difficulty with writing, the teacher can prepare a chart from the child's dictation or the child can use pictures and give information in his own words. Questions asked back and forth by the panel members are beneficial if they are prepared before the discussion so children know what to expect.

Intermediate-grade children need to be cautioned against merely reading their reported information rather than discussing it. A time limit of two to three minutes for each discussant requires the children to be concise and to select the most pertinent information. To increase interest in their discussion, children can use visual aids such as illustrations, transparencies, charts, graphs or a short filmstrip. Points children should remember for any oral presentation are:

(1) Stick to the topic of your report.

(2) Speak clearly and slowly enough to be heard by all.

(3) Use inflections in your voice.

(4) Maintain good eye contact with your audience.

Debates

Debate, to be effective, should be used by intermediate-grade children. They are more capable of the extensive research needed to dig out the pros and cons of an issue. The issue selected for the debate should be one that provokes critical analysis and presents the possibility for taking a position. An example might be: Resolved—The United States Government should spend sufficient funds for research to attempt to send a man to Mars, or, Resolved—The government should pass strict laws governing pollution. Rules should be established for the debate, with time limits set for each presentation and rebuttal. The children should be cautioned about becoming too emotional over the debate. They should understand that a debate is won by presenting the most persuasive argument for their side.

Role-Playing

A historical incident or an attempted solution to a problem can be role-played by a committee. In this activity, the children can use their own language and ideas, based on their research, to depict some incident. Role-playing the signing of the Declaration of Independence or peace treaty talks will help children understand and remember these events. Role-playing gives children the opportunity to express emotions and to attempt to involve themselves in a situation. Children at any grade level can participate in this activity.

TV or Radio Programs

Patterning an oral report after the format of a TV or radio program adds an element of interest. Some children may even add the commercials to make it realistic. Children who have difficulty with oral presentations are often less self-conscious when given the opportunity to pretend to be someone else or to hide behind a microphone.

Show formats such as *This Is Your Life* or *You Were There* are appropriate for historical incidents, while an interview-type format like the *Today Show* is good for factual and opinion reports. The *Walter Cronkite* news format is enjoyed by children for factual reporting.

Dramatic Presentations

Similar to role-playing, but with more definite lines and usually costumes and props, skits and plays can be used by children to present their committee reports. Once again this activity increases the element of interest, and children can hide their self-consciousness behind a character in the play. An example of this type of activity might be a skit depicting a day in the life of a child in Mexico, showing his food, clothing, home and customs. This information is much more easily remembered through visual representation.

The lines for a dramatic presentation can be taped. Children can practice by taping and playing back the presentation until they are satisfied with the performance. Preparation of any oral report can be improved by use of the tape recorder. Each child has the opportunity to hear his mistakes and improve the quality of his voice.

Written Reports

Skills to be developed in the written reports are:

(1) Organize the information in meaningful sequence.
(2) Select the relevant information.
(3) Use correct language, capitalization and punctuation.

The information gathered by a committee can be compiled in a written report when the teacher notes a need for increased skill in this area. The written report might be assembled in a scrapbook with illustrations or in a booklet form. Children can use a textbook format with a table of contents, chapter headings, glossary, etc. All members of the committee should agree on the same format. Reports such as these should be interesting, concise, written in the child's language and available to read. A display of the reports can remain on the reading table until all have had the chance to read them. These reports can also be used for reference when possible.

Graphic Reports

Committees can present their research information through graphic representations. For example, the preparation of a wall mural depicting methods of transportation may be more easily interpreted by children than verbal description. Or the building of a model village may relate more to children about life in Peru than a dozen written reports. The child who is more adept at painting than writing or speaking can meet with success in this type of activity.

SIMULATION ACTIVITIES

Simulations, or simulation games, as they are frequently referred to, present a possible way for more active involvement in learning for the inner-city child. A simulation, through its materials, whether films, tapes, graphic prints or printed material, is intended to re-create a situation as close to a real-life situation as possible. The players take on the role descriptions of the individuals presented in the simulation. A problem with several alternatives (no one is the *correct* alternative) is presented through the simulation for the players to solve. The more sophisticated games produced commercially such as Ghetto and Sunshine (originally for high school, but can be adapted for the elementary school) are aimed at improving racial relations; the City Game[23] gives children the chance to engage in city planning to improve conditions in the city during the next twenty years.

A less sophisticated form of simulation is the role-playing situations developed by Shaftel and Shaftel[24] which are problem stories for children to portray.

Teachers can produce their own simulation games inexpensively and thus build them around the problem areas that are most relevant to their particular classroom.

Games and simulation are purported to be motivating and competitive, and should develop decision-making skills. Research is needed to determine this. One area that particularly needs exploring is that of the lasting effect of game-playing on children. Does it change values? Does it increase competitiveness? What effect does the power to manipulate the lives of others, assumed in a game, have upon children? These are questions that require answers before the effectiveness of games can be determined.

One developer of games suggests "that games about the black community, which are generally written by persons from the suburbs and are based on a series of unfounded clichés about what it is like to be black, not only encourage stereotyping, but create an attitude of condescension toward blacks."[25]

VALUES AND THE INNER-CITY CHILD

Values are either shaped by or reflections of the culture in which we live. "A value system operates for us in at least three ways. First, it serves as a filtration mechanism. . . . Our value system tells us what is important. . . . Second, it serves as a motivating force. . . . Third, a value system, as articulated in language, provides us a conceptual schema for interpreting our environment."[26] The value system of the

---

[23]Glenys G. Unruh, "Urban Relevance and the Social Studies Curriculum," *Social Education* 33 (October, 1969), p. 710.
[24]Shaftel and Shaftel, *Role-Playing for Social Values.*
[25]R. Garry Shirts, "Games Students Play," *Saturday Review* (May 16, 1970), p. 82.
[26]Raymond J. Endres, "The Humanities, the Social Studies, and the Valuing Process," *Social Education* 34 (May, 1970), p. 544.

inner-city child is often different from that which is purported by the school. The teacher must be aware of what the child values and be willing to accept it. It is the teacher's responsibility, however, to assist the child in expressing his beliefs and also help him to determine why he values what he does. The teacher should make him aware of the fact that there are others who hold different values and the reasoning behind these values.

SUMMARY

Social studies offers so much to the inner-city child to help him understand his environment, his problems, the solutions to his problems and to understand himself. The city provides a rich natural laboratory for him to explore if he has the skills and the proper guidance of a good teacher. The child should learn to appreciate his environment while recognizing the tremendous problems that are a part of it. Social studies can help each child to become a knowledgeable citizen—one who is an interested and active participant in the affairs of his world.

Math and Science Programs

Two subject areas that can serve as motivators to increase general interest in school for inner-city children are science and math. These subjects have fewer cultural constrictions than the others. Also, math and science can be learned without the necessity of extensive reading that might hinder the child in other subjects. This should not be misinterpreted—the motivation from math and science should be used to increase interest in reading, rather than using reading (if the child has difficulty reading) to stir interest in math and science.

MATHEMATICS

"Mathematics is not the art of following rote instructions, but is, rather, the art of discovering patterns and finding ways to make use of these patterns."[27]

The real advantages of a mathematics program for inner-city children are (1) math is highly abstract and less culturally conditioned—this may appear as a contradiction to the earlier statements of the importance of concrete experiences; however, this writer suggests that the

---

[27]Dr. Robert Davis, Director of Madison Project, in Stanton W. Webster, *The Disadvantaged Learner*, p. 573.

abstractions of mathematics are quite different from the abstractions of cultures such as the Incas of Peru or the Civil War; (2) it contains fewer derogatory connotations toward race or poverty; (3) success in math increases job opportunities in our technological society; (4) success with math improves self-image; (5) success increases teacher's expectations for the children.[28]

The emphasis in math on inquiry, problem solving and discovery has led to the teaching being more concept-oriented than fact-oriented. In geometry for the elementary grades, figure recognition, pattern recognition, metric and nonmetric geometry, properties of figures and construction are included. There are sufficient visual-manipulative aids available such as sets of plastic 3-D shapes of a cube, cone, pyramid, tetrahedron and cylinder. Algebraic equations and set theory have also become a part of elementary math.

Mathematics is quite different from an arithmetic program and requires more mathematical background than most of the present elementary teachers possess. The teaching of algebra and coordinate geometry to elementary children may require the assistance of high-school math teachers or graduate students from local colleges or universities. Such math programs have been operated quite successfully with inner-city children showing interest and skill in handling abstract concepts in mathematics.[29] However, school systems should pursue the possibility of extensive in-service training of a limited number of teachers (those with some math background and a desire to increase their skills in the area) to serve as resource teachers for the math program.

ARITHMETIC

The regular classroom teacher can do much to enhance the arithmetic instruction (the basic skills). Lack of practicality can be cited as a basic cause for lack of interest in arithmetic. Why should a child fill a page with numerals from 1 through 100 four times? That does become rather boring, and why not use carbon paper if the teacher wants four copies? "No, Johnny, you have your five turned around. . . . Now count those circles one more time." Drill, drill, drill is the cry of the teacher. " Will the child never remember? " What reason does he have for remembering?

---

[28]Ibid., p. 575.
[29]Ibid., p. 579.

Drill is necessary to reinforce the basic skills, but it can be interesting and related to the child's environment. The basic facts for young children can be introduced with concrete materials for counting—blocks, number lines painted on the floor (large enough for child to walk along) Cusennaire rods, pieces of candy (wrapped and later to be eaten), fruit and colored discs. Use every experience for necessary counting in classroom as a resource (lunch count, roll, weather charts, calendar, etc.).

When approaching the problem-solving area—the problems should be realistic. Learn to handle money problems that are actual examples: Our class has five dollars for games and puzzles. How should we spend it? Bring in catalogs with price lists and have children select what they want to buy and fill out the order forms. Large mail-order catalogs can be used extensively in arithmetic instruction.[30] Also newspaper ads of sale items, etc., can be used to discover how much money is really saved on sales. The child should learn how much it costs to charge items.

Take the amount of money the typical family has to spend and determine what the budget should be for food, rent, clothing, etc.

Isn't it more exciting to learn fractions when you are cutting up a pizza, apple, or oranges, although construction paper can be used? Why not discover the area of your classroom, desk, or book rather than a hypothetical field? But have a reason—how much carpeting would we buy for our room, or how much paper do you need to cover your book?

There are numerous games that can be constructed by teachers for arithmetic skills: baseball boards, bingo (addition, subtraction, etc.), puzzles and geoboards to make different shapes.

The intent of this discussion is to emphasize the belief that arithmetic can be interesting and realistic for inner-city children. The teacher should use textbooks as a guide and to provide enrichment activities, but the motivation for arithmetic should come from the activities described above.

SCIENCE PROGRAM

" An elementary science program must be based on the pupil's environment."[31] The environment of the inner-city is not one of but-

---

[30]Ibid., p. 583.
[31]Ibid., p. 596.

terflies and fishes; however, these can become a part of it. Basically
the science program should be based on real problems—where does
the electric light come from? Why does it rain? What happens to the
garbage? How do cars work? These are the questions that come from
the child's environment that he wants answered and he may not receive
answers elsewhere.

Then to extend his environment, field trips, films and filmstrips
can be used, as well as bringing nature and science into the classroom
in the form of living plants and animals, and scientific equipment (not
elaborate or expensive).

However, science should not become a haphazard collection of
materials. The child should practice the skills of the problem-solver:
observing, comparing, interpreting, organizing, hypothesizing, evaluat-
ing, experimenting, testing and generalizing. This means the child needs
manipulative materials to conduct his experiments. For example, the
teacher gives him a magnet and two groups of objects—which materials
can you pick up with a magnet? He tests, draws conclusions and general-
izes at the completion of the experience. Since the child is not seeking
the answer he thinks the teacher wants, the failure factor has been
removed. The results of his experimentation are his answers.

Children become question askers through science experiences;
however, the model provided by the teacher as a question asker is
important. If the teacher's questions are always seeking factual answers,
children think only facts are important. As an example, the teacher
has a picture of the city at different seasons of the year. The teacher
starts the questioning with "Tell me what you see in this picture."
This type of question gives every child the opportunity to answer, since
each can list what he sees in the picture. Then the teacher begins
the process of comparison: "What do you see that is different about
the first picture [winter] and the second [spring]?" After going through
the various comparisons, the teacher asks the child to infer: "Why do
you think these changes occur?" Then the child has an opportunity
to hypothesize and test out his hypothesis. The teacher may introduce
another set of pictures of a city in a tropical zone where the seasons
do not change with question "Why do you think this city is different
from ours?" Thus the child realizes that with the addition of new information it may be necessary for him to change or alter his generalization.
The way the teacher asks the question should be noted: "What do

you see that is different," not "What is different?" or "Why do *you* think" rather than "Why does."

The teacher should motivate for question-asking so that eventually it is the child's questions for which solutions are being sought.

The child can increase his language skills through the recording of his experiments. This should not become a hindrance, however, and it may be necessary for the teacher to be the recorder. For example: the child is observing an earthworm's reaction to heat, light, vinegar and alcohol. A simple chart shows the results:

What happens to the earthworm when it is exposed to:

MATERIAL	REACTION
FLASHLIGHT	
HEAT FROM CANDLE	
VINEGAR	
ALCOHOL	

Conclusion:

The teacher should point out that the scientist works the same way as the child is working when he is searching for solutions to his problems.

One interesting science project in the inner-city has been the developing of kits with science materials to be used by parents and children. The parents come to school on Saturday with their children to participate in the Elementary Science Project. The topics included in these kits are light, color, heat, pressure, friction, nutrition, taste, suction cups, magnets, metals and crystals. The participants learn to observe and record, follow directions, measure accurately and to apply what they learn to daily living.[32] This type of project increases the communication between home and school and increases motivation for learning.

---

[32]Ibid., p. 604.

Science should not be viewed as an opportunity for children to be merely actively doing something; the something should contribute to the child's overall understanding of his relationship to his environment.

The Arts and Physical Education

The arts (music, art and dance) and physical education provide an excellent outlet for the release of emotions and excess energy of inner-city children, as well as to develop their creative ability. Too often insufficient funds are available to provide special teachers in these areas and the classroom teacher is required to provide worthwhile experiences for the children.

CREATIVE EXPRESSION—ART, MUSIC AND DANCE

If a child cannot communicate in an oral or written manner (as is often the situation for an inner-city child), he can express his ideas and feelings in an art form whether it is by the use of art media, music expression, or bodily expression in the form of the dance.

The nurture of creative ability requires a sensitive and understanding teacher and an atmosphere that will provide stimulation of ideas. The tender seed of creativity can die by an insensitive remark or the failure to appreciate what has been created. The child who is always required to color his tulip just as everyone else colors his or reproduce the picture composition directed by the teacher will soon lose the desire to produce his own imaginative ideas. Or the child who is not permitted to create his own dance movements loses interest in following the close directions of a formal dance. A teacher does not need to be talented in the art areas to provide the support and guidance needed by the children in these activities.

Art Activities

Art activities for inner-city children would vary little from those provided for any group of children. A teacher would use the environment to provide the stimulus. For example, the following suggested activities can be planned for the primary and intermediate grades. Note that the activities capitalize on the children's strengths and help to eliminate the problem areas.

Primary: One of the early art activities should be a drawing (use water colors or pastels) of oneself and a drawing of one's family. This gives an overall interpretation of how the child sees himself and his relationship to his family.

Finger painting is good to do since it does not require fine motor coordination. Pictures can depict community or school experiences or can be designs of color.

Finger puppets made from peanuts and scraps of material can then be used with oral language activities. The children should make the puppet characters they want to and dress them as they wish. Here again there should be no cultural barriers since the child can select something from his environment.

An easel with tempera paints, large paper and brushes should be available for children to use to express their ideas after a field trip, a story or some common experience. This should be available for most any grade level. A mural with the interpretation of some experience produced by the contributions of the whole class increases cooperative behavior and the sharing of ideas.

Use scraps of colored construction paper to make designs. The teacher may prepare shapes such as circles, squares and triangles to be pasted on black or gray backgrounds. Or the child can cut out his own desired shapes. Use clay or plasticene to mold figures from their favorite stories or make objects such as pots, ashtrays or spoon-holders.

Obviously, the type of activity described requires the children to draw upon experiences from within their environment.

To motivate children to attempt creative drawings and paintings the teacher should also participate. The child observing a teacher enjoying the designs he produces in finger painting will be much more willing to try it himself. Also, the response of the teacher when a child has completed his drawing or design is important. Permit the child to describe to you what he has completed and then display it along with all of the other pictures of the class. Nothing is so devastating to a child than the failure to have his picture hung with the others. Allow the child to express his emotions in his pictures no matter how violent. It is better to have them appear on the surface where you can discuss them than for these emotions to remain buried to smolder.

Intermediate: The study of primitive art of a culture important to the class—African, Mexican, Aztec, etc.—should stimulate interest in producing similar designs. Also the presentation of the art work of the race or minority groups within the class as black artists, Mexican-American, or Puerto Rican is important for the development of a good self-concept.

The art activities of intermediate children can often be correlated with other areas of study. The production of a rural village when studying Mexico will aid the child in understanding what is the same and different about the village and his city. To relate with past historical events, the pictorial representation of the event in a mural or diorama will certainly make it more concrete.

A continuation of the expressive activities in the form of painting and drawing is just as important for older children. The use of live models for figure drawing of action poses and the use of still-life arrangements for using water colors and pastels is effective. Take the class out into the community to sketch scenes, then take them to some other area of the city for the contrast.

Art activities are most important for inner-city children since they provide an opportunity for success to a child who may not otherwise achieve success in the other subject areas. They also provide an outlet for emotions, ideas and the development of creative talent.

Music and Dance

As indicated earlier, one of the positive factors of the disadvantaged is their love of music;[33] not to stereotype any group, but generally speaking most inner-city children enjoy music. A teacher should capitalize on this if he finds it to be true of his group. Many of these children's homes have loud music playing most of the time. How infrequently though do teachers play music in the background while children are participating in other learning experiences. Music played softly can enhance certain tasks. When a learning task requires much concentration, then music may be a distractor. An example of a time when music may be used would be when the children are copying written work or when the teacher is reading a story or poetry. The music selected should enrich the experience rather than detract from it. Soft music would be used for a quiet and undramatic story while dramatic music heightens the suspense of an exciting or emotional story. Some educators have advocated that these children use music to learn rote exercises such as multiplication tables or spelling words. The individual teacher will need to decide whether this instructional technique is advisable for his particular group. However, he may find it profitable for certain individual children.

Music by artists such as Dionne Warwick, Diana Ross, Stevie Wonder and Jim Brown would be familiar to black children and would relate to their everyday life, just as José Feliciano or Trini Lopez would appeal to Spanish-oriented children. Songs children learn to sing should relate to their culture and environment. Spanish-American children may be more familiar with songs of señors and señoritas using the guitar and accordion than other types of music, while other ethnic groups should learn music related to their culture. This should not be interpreted to mean that only these types of songs should be sung, but certainly some of them should be included.

Children should be given the opportunity to compose their own music with homemade instruments as blocks, drums, sticks and whistles. They will be able to follow their own compositions rather than conforming to established musical patterns, and in turn will learn to appreciate the musical compositions of artists.

---

[33]Frank Riessman, "The Culturally Deprived Child: A New View," *School Life*, XLV (April, 1963), p. 57.

Music related to topics under study, particularly in social studies, is important. To learn the music and dances of a country makes that country appear more realistic; the children have some feel for the flavor of it.

Listening to music for the beauty of the composition is also an experience that should be provided for the children. Music unfamiliar to them can be played in the background first and then later for listening and possible discussion. However, to force a discussion about the selection may spoil the enjoyment of it.

Once again the teacher's pleasure in the music provides an example for the children. Music can definitely enrich the lives of inner-city children and may add the bright spot to otherwise drab experiences.

Interpretive dance can be used with children in kindergarten or earlier and throughout the grades. This experience once again permits the child to express how the music makes him feel. He uses his body to communicate these expressions of feeling to others. Shy children may not respond immediately to interpretive dance and should not be forced to participate. The show-off may become overzealous in his performance but should be ignored unless he is disturbing others. Children can play different characters and interpret how these characters would perform to the music. Examples: How does a tree sway to the music or a frightened child run through the dark? Musical stories can be interpreted through the dance. Comprehension of the story is quickly determined by the child's interpretation of it in dance.

Learning formal dances as square, round and the usual children's dances can be presented if the particular group of children responds to them. Some children are stifled and feel clumsy when required to follow specific dance steps. Since one of the main goals for using dance is to release feelings and excess energies, then it would be wise to refrain from forcing the children into performing these dances. Obviously the teacher should participate in the interpretive dance experiences not as a model to follow, but rather to communicate his own feelings.

PHYSICAL EDUCATION

An important goal of the physical education program is to develop strong and healthy bodies. An organized program of developmental exercises and games geared to the age and maturation level of the children is extremely important to inner-city children. There are few organized activities such as swimming, basketball and baseball for these children, especially in low-income areas as can be found in suburbia. Boys' clubs, community centers and Y groups have tried to provide such activities, but the numbers they reach are limited. Frequently the school serves as a focal point for providing recreational activities.

In addition, why should children be expected to sit in their seats for much of the school day without an opportunity to exercise? A few fifteen-minute breaks per day to complete worthwhile exercises or play games will be most beneficial before going on to instructional tasks. A teacher can readily determine if these exercise breaks are worthwhile for a particular group of children. If the children settle down to work and are less restless when performing instructional tasks, it has been beneficial. However, on certain days it may be necessary to take additional time if the class appears more restless. Teachers should be able to judge the mood of the class and adapt the periods of exercise to times when they are needed.

Children do not need to be taken to the gym to participate in simple exercises such as the jumping jack, touching toes and arm swinging. Teachers can work out exercise routines with the children and then use student leaders. This is another time when music can be used to improve the rhythm of the exercises. These exercises should be completed on a daily basis to provide the most benefits.

Exercises and activities should be planned for younger children to improve their eye-hand coordination, which may aid in the improvement of reading. Bouncing and throwing large rubber balls, skipping and skipping rope, hopscotch and bean bag are a few examples of the type of activity that can be used for this purpose.

Older children enjoy participating in team sports such as volleyball, basketball, baseball and football when sufficient space is available. Strong competitiveness may develop, and care should be exercised to avoid such competition that is unsportsmanlike and detrimental. Healthy competition is good for older children and increases the desire to be proficient in a sport. This author would caution against putting girl teams against boy teams, since the maturity and ability levels vary so between the sexes.

Since many of the children do not have much space to play and often use the streets for their games, the teacher should teach games that can be played in a limited amount of space. This will help the children provide recreational activities for themselves when out of school.

SUMMARY

To provide the inner-city child with activities that will enrich his in-school hours and may enrich his out-of-school hours, music, art, dance and physical education should be an integral part of his school day.

Conclusions

It might be argued that the methods and materials discussed in this book would be advantageous to any child. This argument is probably true, but for inner-city children, they're a necessity.

Any child will progress when nurtured in an environment of respect and understanding, but the inner-city child needs more. He needs enough time, energy and money expended upon him to enable him to develop the full potential of his ability. The dreadful waste of talent from our inner-city schools must be stopped. This can be accomplished only through the development of realistic educational programs provided by teachers with a commitment to and an understanding of the needs of inner-city children.

Children Learn What They Live

If a child lives with criticism,
    He learns to condemn.
If a child lives with hostility,
    He learns to fight.
If a child lives with ridicule,
    He learns to be shy.
If a child lives with shame,
    He learns to feel guilty.
If a child lives with tolerance,
    He learns to be patient.
If a child lives with encouragement,
    He learns confidence.
If a child lives with praise,
    He learns to appreciate.
If a child lives with fairness,
    He learns justice.
If a child lives with security,
    He learns to have faith.
If a child lives with approval,
    He learns to like himself.
If a child lives with acceptance and friendship,
    He learns to find love in the world.

—Dorothy Law Nolte[34]

---

[34]From Sarah Hammond Leeper, *Good Schools for Young Children*, 2nd ed. (New York: The Macmillan Company, 1968). Reprinted by permission of the publisher.

Bibliography

Bereiter, Carl, and Siegfried Englemann. *Teaching Disadvantaged Children in the Preschool.* Englewood Cliffs, N.J.: Prentice-Hall, Inc., 1966.

Cuban, Larry. *To Make a Difference: Teaching in the Inner City.* New York: The Free Press, 1970.

Grambs, Jean D. *Methods and Materials in Intergroup Education: Annotated and Selected Bibliography.* College Park, Maryland: University of Maryland, 1967.

Gross, Beatrice, and Ronald Gross. *Radical School Reform.* New York: Simon and Schuster, Inc., 1969.

Hickerson, Nathaniel. *Education for Alienation.* Englewood Cliffs, N.J.: Prentice-Hall, Inc., 1966.

Holt, John. *How Children Fail.* New York: Dell Publishing Co., Inc., 1964.

Kohl, Herbert. *36 Children.* New York: The World Publishing Company, 1967.

Kozol, Jonathan. *Death at an Early Age.* Boston: Houghton-Mifflin Company, 1967.

Moore, G. Alexander. *Realities of the Urban Classroom: Observations in the Elementary Schools.* New York: Frederick A. Praeger, Inc., 1967.

Passow, A. Harry, Miriam Goldberg, and Abraham J. Tannebaum, eds. *Education of the Disadvantaged.* New York: Holt, Rinehart & Winston, Inc., 1967.

Riessman, Frank. *The Culturally Deprived Child.* New York: Harper & Row, Publishers, 1962.

Taba, Hilda, and Deborah Elkins. *Teaching Strategies of the Culturally Disadvantaged.* Skokie, Ill.: Rand McNally & Co., 1966.

Warner, Sylvia Ashton. *The Teacher.* New York: Simon and Schuster, Inc., 1963.

Webster, Staten W., ed. *The Disadvantaged Learner: Knowing, Understanding, Educating.* San Francisco, Calif.: Chandler Publishing Co., 1966.

Index